Wages & the Law

Jo, Thanks
for your helpful
comments when I
was working on
drafts!
Katie

WAGES & THE LAW

by
KEITH PUTTICK
Senior Lecturer in Law, Staffordshire Polytechnic

with

Richard Painter
Head of Law Department, Staffordshire Polytechnic

Ian Henn
Barrister

and

Stephen Evans
Senior Lecturer in Law, Staffordshire Polytechnic

Shaw & Sons Ltd
Shaway House
London SE26 5AE

Published in February 1989 by Shaw & Sons Ltd. of Shaway House, London SE26 5AE and printed by Richard Clay Ltd., Bungay, Suffolk.

British Library Cataloguing in Publication Data
Puttick, Keith
Wages and the law.
1. Great Britain. Personnel. Remuneration. Law I. Title
II. Painter, Richard W. III. Henn, Ian
344.104'121

ISBN 0-7129-1110-2

© Shaw & Sons Ltd. 1989

The Authors

KEITH PUTTICK is a Senior Lecturer in Law at Staffordshire Polytechnic, and is an occasional lecturer in the School of Management, University of Manchester (UMIST). Before qualifying as a Barrister he worked in employee relations in the engineering industry.

RICHARD PAINTER is Head of the Department of Law at Staffordshire Polytechnic, and is Associate Editor of *Employee Relations*.

IAN HENN is a Barrister, and is a former lecturer in the Faculty of Business and Management, Lancashire Polytechnic.

STEPHEN EVANS is a solicitor, and is a Senior Lecturer in Law at Staffordshire Polytechnic. He is a member of the Law Society's Revenue Law Committee.

CONTENTS

Preface	ix
Bibliography and Abbreviations	xi
1. Introduction	1
2. Employing and paying staff	3
2.1 Possible employment relationships	3
2.2 Possible pay systems	14
2.3 Forms of wages	19
3. Recruitment and commencement	33
3.1 General considerations	33
3.2 Fixing pay levels	34
3.3 Advertisements; pay offers/negotiation; appointments	39
3.4 Discriminatory pay offers and practices	43
4. Wages: contract terms and conditions	50
4.1 General points	50
4.2 Sources of pay terms	51
4.3 Express terms	51
4.4 Implied terms	55
4.5 Rules and notices	58
4.6 Custom and practice	60
4.7 Validity and enforcement of wages terms	61
5. Responsibilities during the contract	66
5.1 Requirement to pay wages	66
5.2 Sick pay/injury pay	71
5.3 Statutory Sick Pay (SSP)	72
5.4 Injuries at work	75
5.5 Pay during medical suspension	78
5.6 Holiday pay	78
5.7 Statutory Maternity Pay	79
5.8 Reduction in work/"lay-off"	84
5.9 Industrial action	91

5.10 Change in working methods; new technology	96
5.11 Time off from work	99
5.12 Miscellaneous wages problems	103
5.13 State assistance with wages	106

6. Changes in wages — 108

Part I. Changes by the parties — 108
6.1 Introductory points — 108
6.2 Permitted variations — 110
6.3 Acceptance without express agreement — 112
6.4 Responses to imposed variations — 114
6.5 Justifying imposed changes — 117

Part II. Changes by virtue of legislation — 119
6.6 Wages Council Orders — 119
6.7 Pay discrimination on race grounds — 121
6.8 Equal pay for women — 122

7. Deductions — 128
7.1 Background: the Wages Act 1986 — 128
7.2 Deductions and payments — 129
7.3 Retail workers — 134
7.4 Court orders — 141
7.5 Tax and National Insurance — 144
7.6 Deducting union subscriptions — 147

8. Termination and wages problems — 150
8.1 Voluntary termination — 150
8.2 Dismissal — 153
8.3 The employer's insolvency — 158
8.4 The transfer of the undertaking — 161
8.5 Frustration of the contract — 163
8.6 Taxation of terminal payments — 166

Index — 169

PREFACE

This book deals with wages issues at each of the four main stages in the employment process: at the outset, when staffing and pay arrangements are being planned; in the recruitment and commencement phase; while the employment continues; and, finally, on termination. Although the primary objective has been to produce a guide to wages law, issues from related areas of employee relations, and the social security and tax systems, have been taken on board where relevant.

Readers who regularly scan the industrial tribunal reports might be disappointed not to see reference to *all* the cases which could have a bearing on wages. Rather than attempting comprehensive coverage, though, the policy has been to get the principles across – and, in doing so, refer to illustrative examples and leading cases on particular points.

The legislative framework of employment law is in a more or less continual state of flux. Provisions in the Employment Act 1988 which have a bearing on the subject have been incorporated into the text. It will be necessary, however, to take note of tax and social security changes since these occur from time to time: and also of only alterations to the figures referred to in the text on matters like trainees' allowances (Chapter 2), statutory sick pay and guarantee pay (Chapter 5), and levels of compensation for unfair dismissal (Chapter 8).

References throughout the book have been predominantly to the male gender, but these should be taken as referring at the same time to the female gender unless otherwise stated (or the context otherwise requires).

I must express our thanks to all the people who have given their time and assistance in different ways. Ron Redgewell and Josephine Robinson for their helpful suggestions on employee relations and contract law points. Sue Morgan and Jacqueline Pate who typed the manuscript and provided much-needed help with the administrative work; and the staff at Shaw and Sons, publishers, particularly Andrew Griffin and Irene Kaplan, for their hard-work and encouragement throughout the project.

Keith Puttick
January 1989

BIBLIOGRAPHY AND ABBREVIATIONS

General Texts

Wedderburn	*The Worker and the Law* (1986)
Smith and Wood	*Industrial Law* (1986)
Bowers	*A Practical Approach to Employment Law* (1986)
Marsh	*Employer and Employee* (Shaw & Sons 1989)
Davies and Freedland	*Labour Law : Text and Materials* (1984)

Specific topics

Recruitment	Newell	*Understanding Recruitment Law* (1984)
Employment contracts	Freedland	*The Contract of Employment* (1976)
	Dix & Crump	*Contracts of Employment* (1980)
Wages Act 1986	Davidson	*A Guide to the Wages Act 1986* (1986)
Personnel/industrial relations aspects	Smith	*The Management of Remuneration: Paying for Effectiveness* (1983)
	Bower	*Handbook of Salary and Wages Systems* (1982)

	ACAS	*Introduction to Payments Systems* (1985)
	Goodman	*Employment Relations in Industrial Society* (1984)
Trade unions	Perrins	*Trade Union Law* (1985)
Fringe benefits	Evans	*Employer's Guide to Fringe Benefits for Employees* (1989)

Reports, magazines, etc.

AC	Appeal Cases
All ER	All England Law Report
CLY	Current Law Year Book
IRLR	Industrial Relations Law Reports
ICR	Industrial Case Reports
ILJ	Industrial Law Journal
KIR	Knights Industrial Reports
QB	Queens Bench Reports
STC	Simon's Tax Cases
TLR	Times Law Reports
WLR	Weekly Law Reports

Courts, legislation, etc.

CA	Court of Appeal
EA	Employment Act 1988
EAT	Employment Appeal Tribunal
ECJ	European Court of Justice
EPCA	Employment Protection (Consolidation) Act 1978
EPA	Equal Pay Act 1970
HL	House of Lords
ICTA	Income and Corporation Taxes Act 1988

RRA	Race Relations Act 1976
SDA	Sex Discrimination Act 1975
SSHBA	Social Security and Housing Benefits Act 1982
SSP (G) Regs	Statutory Sick Pay (General) Regulations 1982, SI 1982/894
TA 1896	Truck Act 1896
TULRA	Trade Union and Labour Relations Act 1974
WA	Wages Act 1986

Chapter 1

INTRODUCTION

The aim of this book is to provide a basic guide to how wages problems are dealt with by the law. Before considering specific matters in later chapters, some general points may be made about the wages system.

The key feature of the system is that an employee is, in most cases, employed under a *contract of employment* (or service). That contract, which contains terms agreed between the employer and employee, will deal with most wages matters from the time the employment commences until it ends. Staff could also be employed as "contractors" under a *contract for services* in suitable cases.

The legal rights and duties of the parties may then be supplemented by *legislation*. Important examples are the Employment Protection (Consolidation) Act 1978 and the Wages Act 1986. The prevailing philosophy though, is against the extension of legislation and government intervention in the employment field, and is in favour of "deregulating" employment conditions as far as possible.[1] This policy can be seen in the main provisions of the Wages Act 1986 (see page 129 below).

The law does not set a minimum wage which applies to all workers, although some industries are still covered by wages council orders. These can fix the minimum basic rates and overtime rates that employers must pay – although they may now be set at levels which are below the national average for the work in question (see pages 119 to 121 below). Until fairly recently unions could apply to have employers' wages brought into line with

---

[1] See, for example, the White Papers *Lifting the Burden* (1985 Cmnd. 9571); and *Releasing Enterprise* (1988 Cmnd. 512)

those generally paid in industry or particular areas,[2] but this has been removed, as have most of the other ways of fixing or maintaining pay levels.

The level of wages which has been offered to, and accepted by, the employee when the job begins will continue to be paid until it is changed (see Chapter 6) or he leaves. While the employment continues there is no general legal requirement on the employer to keep wage levels under review; and unless the contract (or a collective agreement)[3] requires him to renegotiate wages terms, which is unlikely, there is no obligation on him to do so. Nor if negotiations do take place are there any legal rules governing that process (for example requiring the employer to negotiate in "good faith", as in the United States).

Except for exceptional circumstances in which the State may take on some of the responsibilities for wages (e.g. statutory sick pay and lay-off payments, or subsidised employment schemes) the only other State assistance comes through the tax system; or in social security supplements to wages like Family Credit, Income Support, and Housing Benefit.[3]

---

[2] Employment Protection Act 1975, Schedule 11.
[3] Social Security Act 1986 s.20. For guidance, see *Cash Help While You're Working* (DHSS Guidance FB4); and see, further, Chapter 5.13 on these benefits.

Chapter 2

EMPLOYING AND PAYING STAFF

In this chapter we look at the main considerations that must be taken into account by an employer when he is taking on new staff and deciding how to pay them. These points are particularly applicable to those setting up a business for the first time, but they will also be relevant to existing businesses, for example when new departments are set up or staff carrying out new functions are taken on.

The points which an employer must consider can be dealt with under three broad headings. These are:

(2.1) the *type of employment relationship* under which it is intended to employ and pay staff;

(2.2) the basic kinds of *pay system* which can be adopted; and

(2.3) the *form* in which "wages" can be paid, and the advantages and disadvantages associated with the various forms.

2.1 Possible employment relationships

There are a number of employment arrangements in use, and each one has its own particular characteristics which can be significant for wages purposes. Of the types which are referred to below it is notable that the workers in each case are all "employed" in a general sense – otherwise there are important differences between them.

"Employer" and "employee"

This is by far the commonest arrangement as far as most employers and staff are concerned. The employee is employed under a *contract of service* which will normally require the employer to pay wages at regular weekly, monthly, or other periodic intervals which the parties agree on. The employer will be responsible for deducting tax, national insurance, and possibly other contributions (see pages 144 to 149 below) and for accounting for them to the Inland Revenue and other authorities.

For most employers deciding how to employ new staff, the choice of "employee" status will usually be dictated by several main practical considerations:

☐ the need to locate them on one site, and within a single, integrated organisation;

☐ the need to closely supervise their work and to organise their time through the firm's administration and management systems; and

☐ the need to monitor the operation of individuals' and groups' output and performance.

All these criteria can generally be more readily applied, in both legal and practical terms, by employing employees, rather than by using the other main option of "independent contractors" (see below).

Without identifying every type of worker for whom employee status is usually preferable (and whom the tax and other government agencies would normally expect to see employed as employees), it can be said that it ought to be adopted as far as most production staff and staff in office administration are concerned. Examples of staff for whom a "contractor" arrangement may be preferable (for them and for the firm) include part-time staff, particularly if they can work unsupervised, and away from the firm's site; specialist staff, who may also want to work for other firms (see the examples given on pages 6 to 9 and in note 8 below); temporary workers; "consultants" (for example retired or other ex-permanent staff whose services it may be useful to retain); salesmen (although for reasons given on page 17 below the practice is often to employ them under an ordinary contract of service).

The primary objection that some firms have (particularly smaller firms) to engaging "employees" is the cost of wages administration and the on-cost involved in official form-filling, etc. There is also the advantage of flexibility, when employing staff on a casual footing, so that they need only be paid on an *ad hoc* basis and when the work-flow requires this. With firms that *need* such flexibility because of the nature of the business they are involved in, this is obviously a major consideration – particularly given the rule that employees must continue to be paid their normal pay during periods of work shortage (unless contractual powers to "lay off", suspend pay, etc., are clearly set out in their contract or in a collective agreement; for further details and examples, see pages 84 to 91 below).

Another important consideration which the would-be employer should be aware of is that many of the statutory responsibilities on employers apply *only* to this kind of worker. For example, *guarantee payments* (see page 89 below) need only be paid, or given, to "employees", i.e:

> "an individual who has entered into or works under (or where the employment has ceased, worked under) a *contract of employment*".[1]

Similarly *equal pay rights* (see page 122 below) only apply to those "employed" (i.e. employed under a "contract of service" or contract to personally carry out work or labour).[2] *Statutory sick pay* (see page 72 below) need only be paid to an "employee" – somebody working under a contract of service or in an "office", or to whom SSP rights are extended by regulations.[3] Careful reference must be made, however, to the exact scope of the legislation in question. The rights of workers under the Wages Act 1986, for example, are not only given to those working under a "contract of service", but also to:

[1] EPCA s.153 (1). On employee status, see Marsh Ch.2.
[2] EPA s.1 (6).
[3] SSHBA s.26 (1).

> "*any other contract* whereby the individual undertakes to do or perform personally *any work or services* . . .".[4]

Other important rights in relation to wages problems, such as the right to claim for *unfair dismissal*, for example if wages are reduced, or the method of payment is altered (see page 111 below), or on *redundancy* (see pages 86, 98 below), are *also* dependent on the person working as an employee under a contract of employment.

To summarise, the status of "employee", working under a contract of service has its advantages, but may also involve the employer in significant obligations in the wages field. From the worker's point of view – and subject to satisfying any relevant qualifying periods of service, conditions, etc. – it will mean he will be entitled to important statutory payments and other rights.

"Employer" and "contractor"

The next most important option is to employ somebody as a "contractor" or as a "self-employed" person. In this situation the work is undertaken, and pay received, under a *contract for services* – the understanding is that the work is done *independently*, and generally without the individual concerned being part of the "employer's" organisation and under his close supervision. The immediate advantages to an employer are that he is normally relieved of the job of deducting tax and national insurance, and having to make the statutory payments, etc., he would have to make to an employee (discussed above). Benefits like paid holiday leave, sick pay, contributions to pension schemes, etc., which are usually paid to employees are not generally paid to contractors. Whereas an employee's incidental expenses are normally paid (see page 115 below), a contractor's are not.

This sort of arrangement is particularly advantageous where staff will only be engaged for short periods, or

---

[4] WA ss.8 (1), (2), 26 (1).

where it is a small business that needs to avoid the on-costs involved in employing "employees". From the worker's point of view contractor status means he will not enjoy many of the important statutory employment rights of an employee, and for this reason it will usually be less advantageous for most people. On the other hand there may be exceptions, for example where an individual wants to work for more than one employer, or simply prefers the independence that "self-employed" status gives. In tax terms it may be marginally easier to claim deductible expenses,[5] and there are certain advantages for self-employed people and small businesses, particularly in assessing tax liability on setting up or on discontinuance.[6]

Although the parties are obviously free to label the relationship as "self-employed", "contractor", etc., a change to this from employee status is not always legally *conclusive*. A tribunal or court might decide that the individual is, in reality, an *employee* – if he decides to claim for unfair dismissal, or for any of the other rights which only an employee normally receives, or the tax or other authorities decide to challenge a "self-employed" arrangement. There are a number of tests which are used to decide which side of the line such a contested case falls.[7] The following are just some of them:

☐ the extent to which the job is supervised, and the worker's actions are generally "controlled";

☐ whether materials, equipment, etc., are provided by the worker or are provided *for* him;

☐ whether payments are regularly made, and have tax and other deductions taken off, in the way that employee's wages usually are;

[5] Under ICTA, Schedule D.
[6] ICTA Ch. II (ss.60 to 69).
[7] For a more detailed discussion, see Bowers Ch.2; Smith and Wood pp. 8 to 14. Official guidance is published by government bodies. See, for example, *Tax: Employed or Self-Employed?* (Inland Revenue Booklet No. 56 (May 1986)).

- the extent to which the worker is part of the other party's organisation, for example, for the purposes of holiday entitlement, staff schemes, etc.; and
- whether sick pay, or other payments normally made to employees, are given.

Obviously, where the circumstances suggest a measure of independence, it will be easier for the parties to establish a genuine contractor/self-employed arrangement. So, for example, an insurance manager who is paid on commission and may already take on work for other people, could agree with his employer to become self-employed for tax reasons.[8] On the other hand a "self-employed" factory worker who is paid wages without deductions, but who otherwise has all the characteristics of an employee, such as fixed time rates and normal hours, is likely to be treated as an *employee*. He could not be said to be in business on his own account; and if others working with him on similar terms are employed on contracts of employment and are paid PAYE tax this will almost certainly be held to be the case.[9]

"Problem" groups

While most workers fall within either the "employee" or "independent contractor" classification, there are some groups whose uncertain status can cause difficulties when it comes to wages issues. *Crown officers*, for example, are in an uncertain situation as they might not work under any readily identifiable contract, and their terms and conditions can be unilaterally changed. Many of the usual statutory employment rights do, however, extend to Crown employment.[10] *Office-holders* (e.g. club secretaries, Ministers of religion, and some administrative officials) whether appointed or elected to their

[8] *Massey* v *Crown Life Insurance Co.* (1978) IRLR 31, C.A.
[9] *Young and Woods Ltd.* v *West* (1980) IRLR 201, C.A.
[10] See EPCA s.138.

office, may be entitled to remuneration or an honorarium, and other pay entitlements. But these do not necessarily depend on any *contractual* rights. In some cases wages problems affecting them can be dealt with as *if* they were employees (see page 95). *Directors* may be employees and paid under a contract of service, or they may just be paid directors' fees – or possibly nothing at all (see page 56 below). "Employee" status may be difficult to show, though, without a written agreement, unless there is enough evidence to infer a service contract, for example, because of a reference to their salary in the company accounts.[11]

Homeworkers and others who work away from an employer's workplace are frequently employed on a casual basis, and because of their irregular hours, lack of detailed supervision, and uncertain times of payment might at first sight seem to be independent contractors. However, in one important case, it was decided that a shoe-parts assembler working at home, and paid on a piece-rate, was an *employee* employed under a contract of employment. Although the work-flow was sometimes sporadic, there were many other characteristics of the job established over seven years (such as five-day working, provision by the company of materials, etc.) which pointed to employee status.[12] Workers who are in the business of supplying their services only on an irregular basis and without any continuing *obligation* to do so for a particular employer (or corresponding right to be given work) will generally be treated as independent contractors.

Agreements between *family members*, and as *"social" arrangements* between friends, work colleagues, etc., can be problematical as there is a legal presumption (particularly in the former case) that pay arrangements are not legally binding. This applies to agreements for service and services as it does to other types of agreement. The easiest way of overcoming this presumption

[11] *Albert J. Parsons & Sons Ltd.* v *Parsons* (1979) IRLR 117, C.A.
[12] *Airfix Footwear Ltd.* v *Cope* (1978) ICR 1210.

is to make it clear in writing that the arrangement *is* to be legally binding.

"Principal" and "agent"

An agent is simply somebody who has authority from the person who employs him (the principal) to carry out specific functions. This might be a relatively simple, "one-off" task like driving a vehicle to a particular destination;[13] or else be an on-going assignment like acting as a buyer or seller. Although agents are self-employed in a similar way to contractors – so that their duties, remuneration, etc., will be a matter of what has been agreed (in a written or verbal contract) – an "agency" can be created in other ways: for example, where a person has implied or apparent authority to act. If the agent's remuneration has not been specifically agreed he will be legally entitled to reasonable payment for his service.[14]

Agency staff

There may be many areas of a business, particularly in the stages when it is being set up, where casual staff from specialist agencies are invaluable. It is not necessarily clear though – and care is needed in this respect – whether the worker is an employee of the *agency*, or of the *business*. There is legislation[15] which regulates the employment of agency staff, but this is not a point that is covered and may depend on the particular circum-

---

[13] *Ormrod* v *Crosville Motor Services* (1953) 1 W.L.R. 1120.

[14] See, generally, Bowstead *Law of Agency* (15th ed).

[15] Employment Agencies Act 1973, and regulations made under it (particularly the Conduct of Employment Agencies and Employment Businesses Regulations 1976, S.I. No. 715). See generally, on the employment of agency workers, casual staff, and "temps", Newell Ch.2; and Wedderburn pp. 121 to 132.

stances of the case.[16] While the legislation normally requires the agency to make tax and other deductions as the worker's employer, the hiring business may be treated as the employer for other purposes, especially if they are engaged for extended periods of time.

Apprentices and trainees

Entering into apprenticeship arrangements poses no particular problem. If somebody is taken on as an apprentice they will normally be entitled to the benefits and the legal status of an employee [17] except redundancy pay if there is no available work at the end of the apprenticeship. The employer will have to meet the additional cost of providing training and instruction, and it is harder to dismiss an apprentice than other employees. If they are unfairly dismissed their loss of future earnings as a trained worker will be taken into account. National agreements in some industries lay down pay and other terms and conditions which should be applied.

If staff are taken on under government schemes, they may or may not be employees of the business depending on the particular scheme in question and the arrangements made. With earlier work experience programmes like YOPS (Youth Opportunities Programme), the young people involved were not generally regarded as employees because there was no real "employment" relationship between them and the business.[18]

---

[16] Cf *O'Sullivan* v *Thompson-Coon* (1973). XIV KIR 108 where a worker taken on from a relief agency was held *not* to be the hirer's employee, because the business had most of the powers the employer normally has and the worker paid her own N.I. "self-employed" contibutions; and the contract between the hirer and business clearly said she was not the hirer's employee.
[17] EPCA s.153.
[18] *Daley* v *Allied Suppliers* (1983) ICR 90, EAT. EA s26 empowers the Secretary of State to determine the status of trainees.

Under the present *Youth Training Scheme* (YTS) trainees can be offered a contract of employment, either at the start of the training period they are taken on for (normally a two-year or one-year period) or at a later date.[19] The main advantage of employing job starters through YTS is that the bulk of the financial cost is met by the Training Agency (through managing agents). Trainees receive a tax-free minimum basic allowance,[20] and the work they are to undertake, and their training, is discussed with the managing agent.

The main government scheme for adults, which came into operation on 5 September 1988, is *Employment Training*. This replaces some thirty or more existing schemes, but most notably the JTS (Job Training Scheme) and Community Programme. Although trainees can be placed with an employer for practical experience the official view is that they are not "employees", even though they may be under the direction of the firm, etc., they are placed with. The main features of the scheme may be briefly outlined.[21] Trainees are normally drawn from people who have

---

[19] For more detailed guidance on employing YTS trainees, see *Training for Skills - What Every Employer Should Know* (Manpower Services Commission Guide, TFS L3).

[20] Currently £29.50 p.w. in Year One and £35 p.w. in Year Two (on a Two-Year Programme); £29.50 in the first 13 weeks, and £35 p.w. for the rest of the year (on a One-Year Programme). Employers can "top up" these allowances with additional pay. Travelling expenses (if over £3 p.w.) and a lodging allowance may be paid by the M.S.C. to non-employed trainees. The allowance continues for up to three weeks during sick periods, although an employer can make other payments (for example based on his own company sick pay scheme).

[21] For further details, see *A General Guide to Employment Training* (Training Commission publication M10 (1988)). Training Commission Area Offices advise on the operation of the scheme. Most unions and the TUC (formally since 6 September 1988) are not co-operating with the scheme, but have postponed withdrawal from it for two years from that date.

been unemployed for more than six months, although certain other categories may be eligible – e.g. those returning to the labour market after a gap of two years; people with disabilities; those in areas of specific skills shortages; and ex-members of the armed forces. After an initial assessment of individuals' training needs by Training Agents, these are matched with available training opportunities by Training Managers. These may be employers, local authorities, charities, etc., who have contracted to undertake such work with the Training Agency. Apart from a period of approximately 40 per cent of the time spent on directed training (something which is financed indirectly by the Agency, with a small contribution being requested from the employer), the trainee will be engaged on practical work experience in accordance with his or her training "action plan".

Remuneration of Employment Training trainees consists of a training allowance, which is based on normal state benefit entitlements; plus a training allowance of £10 per week. Higher rates of £11.25 and £11.95 apply to certain categories. In addition, training bonuses may be payable from a fund contributed to by the Training Managers, employers and the Agency. Employers can make further payments to trainees, e.g. by paying travel costs or a meal allowance, but they will be advised by Managers on the consequences of this on the trainees' eligibility for State benefits. Other supplements include child care expenses of up to £50 per week for single parents, and travel costs for any excess above £5 per week.

When trainee workers who are not part of a government scheme are employed, an employer may be advised to pay a proportion of the "qualified" rate for the job until the training period is completed. So if, for example, a training period of three years is appropriate the trainee might be paid 70 per cent in year one, 80 per cent in year two, 90 per cent in year three, culminating in the full rate for the job on satisfactory completion of their training. This is commonly provided for in industry-wide national agreements, although it may sometimes be necessary to consult with union representatives and supervisors on the exact training point and wage which is appropriate in a particular case.

2.2 Possible pay systems

The next problem to be addressed is how the staff to be appointed are to be paid. This requires some consideration of the various pay systems in operation. But before that two particular situations must be dealt with. Namely, where *no* wage or system for determining pay has been agreed: and where pay may be linked to the completion of a specific task.

No agreed wages; inadequate wages

It is not essential for a person's wages to be fixed in any particular way before his contract is operative. If no method of calculating wages has been decided on, and there is later disagreement about the wages that are payable, the court can decide what is a reasonable wage.[22] Nor does it seem to matter at all that the employer has contractual rights to decide how much to pay, and when to stop paying it – this is because the courts do not, as a rule, inquire into how adequate the "consideration" for an employment contract is: a point established in the case concerning non-payment of a film actress's pay.[23] A court will look closely, though, at "penalty" terms (e.g. for misbehaviour), or terms which are *so* unfair that they ought not to be enforced, particularly, for example, with children's contracts. In the latter case the court will look at the overall effect of a contract to see if it is beneficial to the child or not.

[22] *Way* v *Latilla* (1937) 3 All E.R. 759. See also the case noted at ff.[42] below.
[23] *Gaumont-British Picture Corporation Ltd* v *Alexander* (1936) 2 All E.R. 1686.

☐ *Example*
An apprentice dancer who was an "infant" was employed under a contract which allowed her dancing master almost complete power over what she did and how much she should be paid. She was also prevented, under the contract, from earning wages for any other employer. The contract was held to be ineffective.[24]

Incomplete performance

Another problem can occur where the employee is taken on for a particular job and he finishes before the work is completed. It is, of course, possible to say that *no* wages are payable if it was clearly intended that *complete* performance was necessary before anything became payable.[25] Unless this *is* clear, though, the employee is entitled to be paid a proportion of the wages contracted for in respect of work completed before he left.[26] For a person working on a time payment system (like a weekly-paid worker; see page 16 below) this would be a payment *pro rata* the wages he would have received for a complete period.

With "lump-sum" contracts the employee (or "contractor") may be able to claim *all* the wages due on the basis that he has *substantially* performed the job contracted for.[27]

---

[24] *De Francesco* v *Barnum* (1890) 45 ChD Reps. 430.Cf, for a case where a contract was held beneficial to the infant, so that a term preventing him from being paid *was* enforceable, *Doyle* v *White City Stadium Ltd.* (1935) 1 K.B. 110.
[25] *Cutter* v *Powell* 101 E.R. 573 (1795); *Vigers* v *Cook* (1919) 2 K.B. 475.
[26] Either on the basis of what is a reasonable amount, or under the Apportionment Act 1870.
[27] E.g. *Hoenig* v *Isaacs* (1952) 2 All E.R. 176 (decorator had to be paid on substantial completion of a job, subject to a small amount being withheld for minor defects).

Systems for determining pay

In practice, an employee's pay is usually determined in accordance with one (or a mixture of both) of the following systems.[28]

☐ *Time rates*. These are usually expressed as an hourly rate, weekly wage, or annual salary – with payments being made weekly in the first two cases and monthly in the case of annual salary. The key feature of time rates is that the employee must be paid at the agreed rate irrespective of individual performance, output, etc.

☐ *Payment by results* (PBR). In this case earnings are determined in accordance with the employee's performance over a given period, and that performance can be assessed by reference to quantity or quality of output (or both). In industrial production jobs, *piecework* is a system commonly used, and basically the employer pays wages at a rate for each "piece" (or other unit of output) produced; or at a rate for the *time* it is agreed should be taken to carry out particular work.

PBR systems can come in many different forms and can be applied to *groups* of workers, for example, a team of assembly workers, or to a group of salesmen covering a particular geographical area. Although an employee's pay may depend entirely on a PBR system, individual contracts and collective agreements can (and commonly do) include a minimum fall-back wage, or combine PBR and time-rate arrangements in systems like measured daywork.[29] Most "white-collar" pay arrangements – for example, schemes for merit and incentive payments, management bonuses, share allocation, etc. – are generally just used to supplement a basic time-rate salary.[30]

[28] See *Introduction to Payment Schemes* (ACAS Booklet No.2) pp. 7 to 20; and on the factors relevant to the choice of payment system see Goodman pp. 91–100. On the "wage–work" bargain, see Davies and Freedland pp. 318 et. seq.
[29] ACAS Booklet, No. 2, p. 12.
[30] See, further, I. Smith Ch.7; and *The Merit Factor: Rewarding Individual Performance* (1985 IPS/IPM).

Most of the legal problems associated with PBR systems arise because of uncertainty over what, precisely, the performance standards are, and how they are to be assessed. The more discretionary or arbitrary the system is for rewarding performance the more likely it is that disagreements may occur (see, for example, the cases referred to in pages 21, 22 below).

To some extent these problems can be overcome by employee participation in managing schemes. This is a feature of many company profit-sharing and share allocation schemes, which, because of their tax advantages are increasingly popular (see pages 28 to 29 below).

An important species of PBR is *commission pay*. Although this is a system which could be adapted for any staff whose performance can be measured in terms of "targets" achieved (several Japanese companies operating in the United Kingdom, for example, apply it fairly widely among their indirect labour-force), it remains particularly relevant to salesmen. Commission systems come in many different forms,[31] and can be set up for employees or contractors (including for example, a salesman employed as an agent). The tendency though, particularly among larger firms, is to employ sales staff under a contract of employment. This has the advantage of enabling the salesman's duties to be closely prescribed within a corporate sales policy and strategy, and gives the firm the flexibility and authority to alter sales targets, commission rates, sales "territories", etc., more easily and at shorter notice than might be possible under other arrangements. It will also usually be more convenient with larger sales forces to set out the remuneration scheme in a single document which applies to all sales staff. The scheme will then be incorporated into the salesman's individual contract. Revisions to the commission arrangements of all the staff can thus be easily made should trading conditions,

---

[31] See, further, *Payment Systems in Britain*, White M. (1981); *Handbook of Salary and Wage Systems* A. Bower (1982); and *Rewarding the Sales Force* (IPM, 1987).

etc., change quickly. It will always be important, though, for clauses in the scheme dealing with the *computation* of commission to be expressed clearly and in detail, especially when the clauses authorise changes that might entail a reduction in earnings.[32]

There will normally be two components to be provided for in a commission pay scheme. Firstly, a basic salary, "retainer", etc., usually paid at fixed intervals, and sometimes linked to administrative or other unmeasured work (for example, in the case of salesmen for "non-sales work" or "non-selling" time). The proportion that this basic salary bears to the total pay package will vary – it may be desirable to increase it if the staff are particularly valuable or to prevent high staff turnover while a business is set up. Secondly, commission payments, paid in respect of targets which have been met and the individual's contribution to sales turnover, profits, etc., measured in accordance with the scheme.[33] Direct selling staff such as car salesmen are often paid for each unit sold and/or on a percentage of the retained profit or volume of sales over a given period. An element of remuneration can be paid in advance, for example for "expenses" or in respect of anticipated "repeat" sales to regular customers.[34] Com-

---

[32] See *R. F. Hill Ltd.* v *Mooney* (1981) IRLR 258 (discussed page 111 below).

[33] If a minimum level of earnings is specified, or was envisaged by the parties, then sufficient opportunity to *achieve* those earnings must be given : otherwise the employer may be liable to pay them anyway; see *Bauman* v *Hulton Press Ltd.* (1952) 2 All E.R. 1121.

[34] Employers should take care to deal with the possibility of *overpayment* of advance commission and expenses because the courts will not readily *imply* any obligation to make repayments; see *Clayton Newbury Ltd.* v *Findlay* (1953) 2 All E.R. 826 (where the court refused to order repayments where advances of expenses exceeded commission earnt). Cf., though, *Bronester Ltd.* v *Priddle* (1961) 3 All E.R. 471 (where it was held that commission advances *did* have to be paid under the contract).

mission can be paid individually or distributed among a group.

In setting up such systems, and to avoid potential legal pitfalls, it is essential to provide for a fair system of review of performance, and to clearly identify the possible sanctions for non-performance. If there are factors that can adversely affect earnings that are beyond the firm's or the individual's control, these must be catered for. Finally, it is important to note that commission contracts (whether those of an employee or contractor) are subject to an implied term that there will be sufficient work provided to enable the individuals to make a living.[35]

This obligation could be displaced, however, by clauses in the contract dealing with situations where work is not available.

2.3 Forms of "wages"

The Oxford dictionary defines a wage as a "payment to a person for service rendered". This might simply be a "one-off" payment, but more usually it takes the form of *regular periodic payments* to an employee, and by far the majority of workers are paid in this way, at either weekly or monthly intervals.

In addition to a basic payment, wages can also include benefits which can be cash payments (like bonuses, assistance with housing costs, etc.). Or they might be non-cash benefits, like payments into a private medical insurance scheme, use of subsidised canteen, and so forth. The advantages and disadvantages of paying particular benefits – particularly given the tax implica-

[35] The main case is *Turner* v *Goldsmith* (1891) 1 QB 544 (after two years of a five year commission contract the employer's works burnt down – as there was no provision dealing with this eventuality the employer remained liable for payment for work which had not been provided); on implied terms see pages 55 to 58 below.

tions in each case – are discussed below. Before that a number of more general points about wages should be made.

Is the payment, benefit, etc., a "wage"?

Although most of the payments received by an employee might be regarded as wages or pay, the *law* does not necessarily treat them as such. For the purposes of most wages legislation the general rule is that the payment must be clearly referable to the employment – if it has been made for some *other* reason then it may not have the main characteristic of wages, namely, that it is the "consideration" or price paid for services rendered. Thus, for example, the payment of sums just to induce staff to take on a different type of employment would not necessarily be charged to tax as an emolument from employment.[36] The question may depend, though, on the particular legislation in question. So "tips", for example – paid by customers to a waiter (and then paid, in part, over to the employer) – have *not* been regarded as "wages" for the purposes of requiring the employer to provide an itemised pay statement.[37] On the other hand tips *are* treated as part of the employee's earnings when it comes to working out how much pay he normally receives.[38]

The fact that payments are not paid *directly* to the employee is generally irrelevant for the purposes of most wages legislation so long as he receives a tangible benefit at some stage. There has been some doubt about employers' contributions to schemes (like retirement schemes) which are jointly funded by employers and employees, but because these have conferred benefits which are clearly referable to the employment, they have

---

[36] *Vaughan-Neil* v *I.R.C.* (1979) STC 644; (1979) 3 All E.R. 481.
[37] *Cofone* v *Spaghetti House Ltd.* (1980) ICR 155.
[38] *Manubens* v *Leon* (1919) 1 K.B. 208 (hairdresser's assistant's tips, as well as weekly wage, taken into account).

generally been treated as wages or "pay" for most wages purposes.[39]

"Contractual"/"non-contractual" wages

A question that crops up regularly is whether a particular payment or benefit is "contractual" in the sense that it *must* be paid as a contractual obligation. In certain circumstances payments (or the promise to make them) may *not* be contractual. The point is an important one in many different wages contexts. It is clearly essential in deciding what the employee's correct pay is when it is due or when it is later claimed in legal proceedings. But it is also something which frequently comes up when calculating a "week's pay" – a concept that runs throughout employment legislation. It is used for determining what an employee is deemed to normally earn[40] when working out statutory entitlements like guarantee payments, compensation for redundancy, etc., referred to later in this book.

It is clearly desirable to try to avoid uncertainty or any ambiguity at the time the employee is taken on. If there is any argument at a later stage, though, it will obviously be necessary to look at any written or other evidence of what the parties intended. Thus, a promise to pay a salary plus "such bonus (if any) as the directors . . . shall from time to time determine" would usually refer to nothing more than a *discretionary* (or "non-contractual") payment.[41] On the other hand a promise to pay a bonus to replace the annual pay rise has been held to create *contractual* rights:

---

[39] See *Worringham and Humphreys* v *Lloyds Bank Ltd.* (1981) IRLR 178 (ECJ); (1982) IRLR 74, C.A.
[40] EPCA Schedule 14, Part II; and c.f. Marsh Appendix II.
[41] *Lavarack* v *Woods of Colchester Ltd.* [1967] 1 Q.B. 278, C.A. A notice that sick pay was only paid *ex gratia* is decisive; *Petrie* v *MacFisheries Ltd.* (1939) 4 All E.R. 281, C.A.

☐ *Example*
A secretary was told in a letter that she would receive, instead of an annual rise, "a bonus on the net trading profit . . . an amount according to the trading results of the previous financial year . . ." It was not stated any more clearly, though *how* the bonus would be calculated. After paying bonuses for several years the payments ceased. It was held that the letter established more than simply a discretion to pay or not pay unspecified amounts. It created an *entitlement* which should be a reasonable sum, taking into account what would have been paid in an annual rise and what would be reasonable additional remuneration in relation to trading profits.[42]

"Extra responsibility" payments (and similar payments) are often treated as just discretionary supplements to basic pay, but they can still cause problems if they are discontinued or their value diminishes.

☐ *Example*
P was a headmaster who was given additional payments to reflect special duties and responsibilities. This was fixed at 62 per cent of the assistant teachers' level of payment for additional responsibilities. When the assistant teachers' payment was renegotiated and increased, P's payment was not increased proportionately. The payment was held not to be a contractual entitlement and the local authority employer was not, as P claimed, obliged to pay it until his retirement as if it were part of his salary.[43]

Choosing how to pay wages; tax considerations

When employing staff the prime consideration is to minimise the costs involved in providing remuneration, and this involves careful consideration of the adminis-

---

[42] *Powell* v *Braun* (1954) 1 All E.R. 484.
[43] *Smith* v *Stockport M.B.C.* 8 August 1979 (1979) CLY 905.

trative costs associated with providing particular forms of wages. In most cases, wages or salary are paid in money, though there can be income tax and other advantages for the payment of at least part of the wages in "kind". Employees are taxed on their wages (or emoluments) under Schedule E of the Income and Corporation Taxes Act 1988 (ICTA).[44] For this purpose, *emoluments* includes all "salaries, fees, wages, perquisites and profits whatsoever".[45] For wages paid in money, the income tax rates (after deduction of any available personal reliefs of the employee) are applied to the gross amount and tax deducted in accordance with the rules explained in Chapter 7. Where the employee agrees to accept part of his wages in "kind", the tax system adopts different rules depending upon the type of benefit or "perk" conferred. Although the general rule is that *all* emoluments of the employment paid in money or money's worth are liable to income tax, in some cases, the "perk" may be completely free of tax, whereas in others it may be taxed at a low value.

This area of law is one of some complexity and for the precise tax treatment of particular benefits reference should be made to recognised tax works.[46] However, the remainder of this Chapter will be devoted to an outline of the tax treatment of the more common forms of benefit in kind in order to illustrate the incentive for employers and employees to negotiate for payment of part of the agreed wages in this form.

☐ *Note*

For many benefits in kind, the tax system distinguishes between two categories of employee. Firstly, there are the so-called "higher paid" employees (also

---

[44] ICTA s.19. Payments to self-employed workers are liable to income tax under Schedule D Cases I & II.
[45] ICTA s.131.
[46] For a useful guide to planning employee remuneration, see Tolley's *Tax Planning* (1988, Vol.1), pp. 205 to 222; and Tolley's *Income Tax 1988-9* (which are updated annually).

known as P11D employees[47]) whose earnings, inclusive of perks, amount at present to £8500 or more. These employees are subject to a special tax code for their benefits in kind which previously may have escaped tax.[48] In most cases the employee will be taxed on the cost to the employer of providing the benefit.

Secondly, for the residual class of employees on lower earnings levels, many benefits are only taxable if capable of being converted into money.[49] The following categories of benefits in kind contain illustrations as to the operation of this "convertibility" test.

Cars

The provision of a company car is probably the most common form of benefit in kind, though it is normally only appropriate for more senior staff or employees whose duties require the provision of transport. Higher paid employees are taxed by reference to a statutory scale[50] and the taxable figure is determined by the age, value and engine capacity of the car. For example, on current figures, the salesman who is provided with a new 1.6 litre Vauxhall Cavalier, and who is allowed unrestricted private use is taxed on £1400. This means that if he is a basic rate taxpayer he must pay income tax of around £6.73p per week for his car. The income tax bill is halved if the employee travels more than 18,000 business miles during the tax year but is increased by 50 per cent if the employee travels 2500 or less business miles in the vehicle. If the salesman is also given free petrol for his private motoring he is taxed on a similar basis on this benefit too.[51]

[47] Named after the income tax form the employer must complete for staff in this category.
[48] ICTA ss.153 to 168. Note that this category of employee also includes directors whatever the level of their salary.
[49] *Tennant* v *Smith* (1892) AC 150.
[50] Income Tax (Cash Equivalents of Car Benefits) Order 1988.
[51] On current figures the salesman would pay tax of £2.88 p.w. for the vehicle in question.

For lower paid employees the benefit of a company car is completely tax free as it is not regarded as capable of being converted into money. Clearly the employee cannot sell the vehicle as it does not belong to him, nor for the same reason can he hire it out to his friends. It does not matter that the employee makes a notional saving in not having to provide his own vehicle.

In each case there is a distinct advantage for the employee who is spared the cost of providing, insuring, repairing and servicing his own motor vehicle. Any liability to tax is easily outweighed by the freedom to invest his resources more profitably and avoid the inevitable depreciation inherent in the purchase of a motor car.

Expense accounts

Formerly it would be common for certain senior employees to be given remuneration in a disguised form via an "expense account". For example, the employee might be given £5000 for expenses but where it was understood that the genuine business expenses would only form part of this amount leaving the balance as a tax free profit for the employee. The law is now more strict in the regulation of these payments and for higher paid employees, any expenses paid to the employee or put at his disposal are treated as part of his salary. The employee can, however, deduct any genuine expenses provided they satisfy stringent conditions.[52] The net result is that genuine payments for expenses are effectively ignored by the tax system leaving only the excess exposed to taxation. For lower paid employees, provided the expense payments are merely in re-imbursement of money spent on behalf of the employer, such payments are not normally taxable.

---

[52] ICTA s.198 where the expenses, to be tax deductible, must be incurred wholly, exclusively and necessarily in the performance of the employee's duties.

Living accommodation

Whilst less common for the majority of employees, the provision of living accommodation such as a rent-free flat or house can nevertheless be regarded as a valuable perk. Basically, the employee (whether or not he is higher paid) is taxed on the "annual value" of the premises based on a formula almost exactly the same as that for calculating the rateable value of property.[53] Any rent he pays to the employer is then deducted from this amount and he is only taxable on the balance.[54] In fact the benefit can be tax free altogether if provided for caretakers and security staff or similar where living in job-related accommodation is necessary or customary. Though treated favourably in the hands of the employee, a major disadvantage for the employer is the fact that large amounts of capital may be tied up in the provision of housing where the money could be more profitably employed in the business. Additionally, in times of rapidly increasing house prices, employees are better advised to puchase their own homes in view of the favourable tax climate created by mortgage interest relief and the capital gains tax exemption for private residences.

Vouchers

Some employees receive extra rewards (usually as part of a bonus scheme or similar) by the provision of vouchers[55] or credit tokens which may be exchanged for

---

[53] ICTA ss.145, 146 and 837. The rateable value of residential property is notoriously low and the amount of income tax paid for such a benefit will be small compared to the amount saved by the employee in not having to provide his own accommodation.

[54] There is an extra tax charge on the employee if the employer's cost in providing the property exceeds £75000.

[55] Defined as a "voucher, stamp or similar document or token" – ss.141 to 143 ICTA.

cash or goods and services, for example a free holiday. Employees who receive these benefits as part of their remuneration package are now generally taxable on what it cost the employer to provide the vouchers. For example, if an employer buys holiday vouchers at a cost of £1500 to reward the top salesman, the latter will be taxed as though he had received a salary increase for this year of £1500. It must be remembered that at the basic rate of income tax, currently 25 per cent, the salesman will actually pay £375 extra in tax – far less than if he had paid for the holiday out of his own resources. Furthermore, if the salesman had demanded a pay rise to enable him to pay for such a holiday himself the cost to the employer would have been £2000.[56]

Interest-free or cheap loans

This form of perk has gained increasing popularity with employers, particularly in the South-East, where recently it has been difficult to attract employees to move south in view of the high cost of housing and commuting. Interest free loans may be given for the purchase of, for example, a railway season ticket, commonly costing up to £2000. For more senior employees, moving into a high cost housing area, an interest free loan can be made to assist them in purchasing a comparable house. In either case, the law distinguishes again between the higher paid employees and others. For the former, interest free or cheap loans are, on the face of it, taxable on a notional rate of interest, currently 13.5 per cent.[57] There are, however, exceptions which, in many cases will avoid any charge to tax. Firstly, an interest free loan is tax free if the taxable amount is under £200. At current rates this covers loans up to around £1450. In

[56] I.e. the sum which, after payment of tax at 25 per cent, leaves enough to pay for the holiday.
[57] ICTA ss.160 to 161 and Income Tax (Official Rate of Interest on Beneficial Loans) Order 1987. This rate can change often in response to general interest rate changes.

addition, a loan is tax free if it would have qualified for income tax relief in any event. This has the effect of exempting loans up to £30000 for the purchase and improvement of property which is a main residence.

Once again, it must be pointed out that even if the loan is taxable, the net cost to the employee is only around 2.5 per cent of the loan. Had he borrowed the money from his bank at market rates he may be paying interest often in excess of around five times this amount. Better still for the lower paid, any interest free loans for the specific purposes referred to are always regarded as tax free.

Employee share schemes

In recent years, it has become fashionable amongst limited companies to reward employees by the use of employee share schemes. Not only do these enjoy favourable tax status where Inland Revenue approval is obtained but they are seen as promoting loyalty and incentives for staff participating. The conditions for approval are complex and reference should be made to specialist works[58] but briefly there are three types of scheme[59] which, in reverse order of popularity, are as follows:

☐ *Profit sharing schemes*
  Here, trustees are given funds by the employing company in order to purchase the company's shares which are then held on behalf of the employees. To secure Inland Revenue approval *all* employees must be able to participate and the market value of the shares appropriated to each employee per year cannot exceed a certain limit (£1250 or 10 per cent of the employee's emoluments to a limit of £5000). The shares must then be retained by the trustees for at least two years. The tax advantage of the arrangements is that the employees are not taxed on the

[58] See e.g. Tolley's *Tax Planning* (1988 Vol. 2) pp. 803 to 845.
[59] ICTA ss.185 to 186.

receipt of the shares and are only taxed on any profit made when they are eventually sold.

☐ *Savings related share option schemes*
These schemes are funded by the employees under "Save As You Earn" contracts and the maximum monthly contribution is currently £100. Upon the maturity of the SAYE contract, usually after five to seven years, the employees can purchase shares in their company at a fixed and generally favourable price without any liability to income tax.

☐ *Share option schemes*
Under share option schemes, employees (in practice normally restricted to senior executives) are granted an option to purchase the company's shares at a price fixed by reference to the market value on the date of the grant. The option can then be exercised by the employees any time between four and ten years from this date and in most cases the value of the shares will have risen sharply. The only tax effect of this scheme is that capital gains tax is payable on the profit made by the employee on a subsequent sale of the shares. Though large profits can be made by the employees with little financial risk, it is thought worthwhile to offer such employees this performance related incentive which, by preventing them from exercising options for at least three years, promotes loyalty and longevity of service.

Profit related pay

A novel device as part of the Government's continuing strategy to provide incentives for employees, was the introduction in 1987 of "Profit Related Pay".[60] This is particularly useful for unincorporated businesses who are not able to offer their employees the benefits of the share schemes outlined above. Though any employer

[60] Now contained in ICTA ss.169 to 184.

has always been able to negotiate wages with a performance related element, for example, commission or piecework, the significance of the current scheme is that the profit related portion of wages is subject to only half the normal rate of income tax. It goes without saying that the Government cannot allow *all* an employee's wages to receive such favourable tax treatment. A maximum limit of £3000 or 20 per cent of salary (whichever is lower) has therefore been imposed for the profit-related element of salary. In practice this means a maximum tax saving of £375 for a basic rate taxpayer at current rates. On the other hand, the employee must always remember that under this scheme up to 5 per cent of his earnings could go down as well as up!

Pensions

Most employees nowadays will belong to a pension scheme usually arranged by the employer to which contributions will be made by both employer and employee.[61] More fortunate employees may belong to a non-contributory scheme where all contributions are paid by the employer. The contributions are made to a fund administered by trustees who are then responsible for investing the fund and paying out pensions. These occupational pension schemes, once approved by the Inland Revenue,[62] receive favourable tax treatment and form an important element of an employee's remuneration package. The current rules provide that payments by the employer to such a scheme (and for which there is no upper limit) do not form part of the taxable emoluments of the employee and this constitutes a valuable benefit. This is clearly advantageous as the contributions can be invested free of tax[63] and a lump sum, also

---

[61] The employee receives tax relief on his own contributions up to a limit of 15 per cent of his gross emoluments.
[62] Under ICTA ss.590 to 596.
[63] Neither income tax nor capital gains tax is payable on the investments in the fund.

free of tax to a certain limit, can be paid to an employee upon retirement provided certain conditions are satisfied.

Miscellaneous

Though the list above deals with many of the common forms of benefit it is not exhaustive. The employer may decide to reward his employee by discharging one of the employee's personal debts, for example his rates bill. Provided this is intended as a reward, the employee will be taxed as though he had received the amount as wages.[64] As for the holiday example mentioned above, the employee is only worse off by the amount of income tax he must pay on this figure – 25 per cent (at present) if he is a basic rate taxpayer. In a similar vein, higher paid employees who receive free membership of a private health insurance scheme or whose children receive scholarships from the company are taxed on the cost to the employer in each case.[65]

A novel form of perk concerns the loan of assets to employees, for example video equipment or even clothes! Lower paid employees would generally not be taxed on these benefits[66] (even though they are spared the expense of providing such articles for themselves) and higher paid staff are only taxable on 20 per cent of the market value of the goods. Thus, if a video-camera costing £1000 is loaned to an employee earning more than £8500 per annum he will only be taxed on £200 for each year of the loan. At the basic rate, income tax on this useful perk is less than £1 per week.

Finally, a consideration of benefits in kind would not be complete without a mention that luncheon vouchers provided by an employer are, by concession, tax free up to the princely sum of 15 pence per day![67]

[64] *Nicoll* v *Austin* (1935) 19 Tax Cases 531.
[65] ICTA ss.154 and 165.
[66] See the "convertibility" test above.
[67] Inland Revenue Concession A2.

Summary

In all cases, the employer and employees should be aware of the income tax implications before finalising negotiations on wages. From the examples seen above, in many cases a lower tax bill for the employee can be achieved by the judicious use of a benefit in kind rather than a cash payment to the employee. Additionally, the employee's perception of the value of the benefit is often greater than the net cost to the employer.[68] Furthermore, the employee's National Insurance contributions are generally only assessed on the amount of monetary payments. On the other hand, there is an inevitable administrative headache if employers negotiate separate remuneration packages tailored to the needs of each employee and in practice such individual attention will only be given to senior or key personnel. Finally, it must always be remembered that the employee who receives a low monetary salary made up with a comprehensive package of perks may be disadvantaged when it comes to calculating salary for mortgage purposes or pension entitlement as generally both calculations only have regard to the actual salary level. There are also a number of state benefits which can be claimed by both full and part-time staff which are discussed in Chapter 5.13 below. These may, of course, be relevant in wages planning.

---

[68] E.g. the provision of free legal services for the employees of solicitors, or free travel for the employees of airline companies.

Chapter 3

RECRUITMENT AND COMMENCEMENT

3.1 General considerations

The stage at which new staff are recruited and start work is one which contains a number of dangerous pitfalls as far as wages are concerned. Whether the staff are being recruited to a new business, or are additions or replacements to an established one, these dangers are avoidable if sufficient care is taken. Before turning to the specific aspects of this area which require detailed attention, some general observations can be made.

In general terms an employer is free to advertise, negotiate on, and then offer whatever wages terms and conditions he thinks fit in order to obtain the staff he requires. The main limitation on this freedom is where provisions dealing with these matters are in national or local pay agreements; or where more informal procedural arrangements operate, for example requiring prior consultation with union officials. Although there are still some important legislative restrictions and safeguards for employees that operate (these are dealt with later in this chapter), the present political and economic environment is one which favours a "free market" approach to fixing pay levels.

While Parliament could, of course, apply controls over pay offers, and wage movements generally, as it has done before (for example during wartime, or as an aspect of counter-inflation policy) – in which case previous court decisions, etc., may become relevant again[1] – the most important ground rules are now, for the most part, catered for by the ordinary principles of contract.

---

[1] See pages 62 to 65 below.

These will be of particular relevance to a would-be employer who has to recruit staff with bargaining power, and who are looking for the best conditions they think they can obtain – sectors like financial and computing services, where there is a high turnover of staff, and where skills are in a high demand, are prime examples. But, even where, as in the majority of cases, there is little or no preliminary bargaining, it is still imperative to be familiar with the basic principles governing offer and acceptance.

The *first* step, though, in the recruitment process is to carefully identify all the key elements of the job to be done (in a draft "job description"); and then to make an initial determination of what it will cost, in pay terms, to recruit and retain a suitable job-holder.

3.2 Fixing pay levels

In deciding the pay terms on which to recruit, an employer must have regard to a variety of legal and industrial relations considerations. If he is setting up a business from scratch he will obviously enjoy greater freedom to devise pay systems and fix wages than if he is recruiting within pay structures which are already in operation. In either case the following points should be noted:

☐ staff of the kind which it is proposed to recruit may be subject to a *wages council order*, in which case they will have to be paid above a legally-prescribed minimum rate (see further pages 119 to 121 below). Advice on this can be obtained from the Department of Employment and Wages Inspectorate;

☐ recruitment practices (including the terms on which employment is offered and given) which *discriminate* are illegal (see pages 39 to 49 below). At present this is concerned with grounds of race and sex, but it is not inconceivable that other "isms" – "ageism" and the linking of pay levels to age, for example – may attract Parliament's or the EEC's attention;

☐ *overseas workers* generally require a work permit, and a condition on granting them is that the pay offered is not substantially below the "going rate" for such work. Application forms are issued by Department of Employment offices. EEC nationals do not require permits;

☐ *employment agencies and businesses* are required to comply with regulations which, among other things, deal with pay offers and the provision of detailed information to workers about pay and conditions, the work involved, etc.;[2]

☐ *employers that are statutory bodies* (like local authorities, nationalised industries, etc.) may be restricted by expenditure requirements and audit rules over the pay levels at which they can employ staff (see page 63 below); and

☐ the government may be operating an *"extra-legal"* policy on employment conditions, for example in relation to staff working on defence procurement contracts, or the employment of young people in city areas.[3] Although sanctions in this case may not be "legal", they may nevertheless be significant enough not to be ignored.

New businesses

In the case of new enterprises the main points to take into account[4] will include:

---

[2] Employment Agencies Act 1973 and regulations made thereunder; the Conduct of Employment Agencies and Employment Businesses Regulations 1976 S.I. No. 715.
[3] Reported in *The Times* 24 June 1986 and elsewhere.
[4] For guidance, see ACAS guides *Employing People* (1987); *Employment Policies* (1986); *Recruitment and Selection* (1986).

- ☐ the *rates being paid to similar workers nationally and locally*. Information on this can be found in newspapers and journals in which there are advertisements for comparable staff; from the Department of Employment and Job Centres; and from relevant trade associations and Chambers of Commerce;

- ☐ the need to pay similar or comparable benefits as paid by *competitors*; especially if they operate locally and are in the business of "lifting" other firms' staff!

- ☐ any *collective agreements that operate for the industry concerned*. If it is decided to recognise a union as a body which will represent the staff,[5] it will be possible to either:

    (a) state in each individual's letter of appointment and statement of terms (see page 52 below) that terms and conditions will be in accordance with an established *industry-wide agreement* (and any changes that may be made to it from time to time).[6] In this case it will obviously be desirable for the employer to join the employers' association or bargaining body which negotiates the agreement, for the purposes of receiving information about wages in the industry and participating in the bargaining process. Similarly, staff will want to do the same on their side;

    (b) state that the terms and conditions will be in accordance with a *locally-agreed agreement* made (and revised from time to time) between the employer and union (or staff association) representatives employed by the employer. The obvious

---

[5] There is no legal obligation to recognise a union. If it *is* recognised – either in a formal agreement or as a matter of practice – recognition can be for all or just *some* pay purposes. See further on this, Perrins *Trade Union Law* pp. 236 to 238; and Marsh

[6] On the way in which an individual's contractual terms can be incorporated from collective agreements, etc., see pages 54 to 55 below.

advantage here (compared with simply adopting existing conditions) is that a new employer will be able to have far greater control, both when *establishing* collective pay arrangements for his workforce, and when it comes to *revising* them.

In either case the main advantages of collective arrangements, particularly where large groups of staff are involved, is that the problems of having to bargain on an individual basis on "core" salary structure and other pay matters is avoided – both at the recruitment stage and later. This can be done while at the same time introducing a certain amount of individual pay or benefits diversity, for example, in the form of intra-grade payments for extra responsibility, "merit" payments, etc., which do not make a significant impact on basic rates agreed for each job, or which have been produced by job evaluations;

☐ *rates that are paid to specialist staff*. Such staff may have professional bodies which give their members and employers guidance on pay matters. Although a would-be employer is not bound to pay in accordance with such guidance, it may be unwise not to do so if staff are later going to be tempted to leave for better conditions elsewhere.

Existing businesses

As far as recruitment to existing enterprises is concerned, similar considerations will often apply. As to the third point, it may be possible to *extend* existing union or staff association representation to staff of the kind to be recruited. This will depend, though, on whether the union in question is appropriate to represent such staff; and whether there are satisfactory agreements on pay, etc., already in operation which *could* extend to them. In any case it is always possible to establish a *new* local agreement in conjunction with existing staff representatives (or officials from a new union that is appropriate),

37

and then recruit staff into the agreed new structure.[7]

It will always be necessary to consider an appropriate "rate for the job" after taking into account the rates already paid to staff doing the same or similar work.[8] Particular care is needed if there is any danger of affecting existing pay differentials and relativities as between individuals or groups of workers within the enterprise (including associated companies). These may just present *industrial relations* problems, but it is *also* possible that differentials and relativities are formally established in a collective agreement (or possibly an individuals' contracts) and thus give staff *contractual* rights. Care must also be taken to ensure that introducing a new pay scheme does not mean that some staff, whether the existing or new staff, are paid differently, despite doing similar work. The danger here is that to do so may give rise to equal pay claims (see pages 122 to 127 and 43 below).

Many of the problems associated with differentials and relativities can be avoided where there is a formal collective agreement (or company salary plan, etc.) in operation which deals satisfactorily with staff appointments and pay progression. Even where such an agreement, or plan, is not in operation it will still be necessary to ensure that new staff are being placed at the right grade or point within the existing pay structure. Whether there is a pay agreement or not it is always appropriate to consider a training rate, especially for inexperienced staff and those requiring supervision or job instruction. Finally, even if an agreement does not provide for it, it is always advisable to consult with any staff who have a legitimate interest in new appointments, including supervisors and staff representatives. This should be done at as early a stage as possible, i.e.

---

[7] Although "single union" pay bargaining arrangements are usually desirable, in practice their establishment or retention can be difficult, especially when unions are competing for negotiating rights.

[8] See, further, ACAS *Recruitment and Selection* p.7.

before advertisements are placed, if pay problems are anticipated.

3.3 Advertisements; pay offers/negotiations; appointments

Advertisements

Once a possible pay "package" has been formulated and, if this has been necessary, a salary scheme has been devised and introduced, the next step will be to advertise for staff. In the case of an established business *internal* advertising of new jobs, say for a period of two weeks prior to advertising can, of course, result in significant savings on advertising and other recruitment costs. Recruitment and promotion from within an enterprise can also mean savings on the wages bill if it obviates training overheads, for example on induction programmes. On the other hand it may be more cost-effective in the longer run to recruit from outside if this is the only way to obtain the right staff for the work.

Whether internal or external advertising is used, it is important that any information provided about pay and benefits is *accurate*. If it is not, and there is any doubt later about the precise pay terms on which the person is working, the contents of the advertisement could be decisive.[9] This would be the case, for example, where there was no later letter of appointment, or else the letter did not deal sufficiently clearly with a contentious point. There is no obligation, however, to provide any detailed information about pay at the advertising stage. Indeed, unless the firm is confident that the specific salary or package offered is going to produce sufficient applications, there is a lot to be said for simply expressing the salary as "negotiable" or linking the pay that will be

---

[9] See *Pedersen* v *Camden, London Borough Council* (1981) ICR 674; IRLR 173; and see, generally, on advertising jobs, Newell Ch.3.

offered to experience and qualifications. If there are any unusual and attractive parts of the pay package, for example "non-contributory pension" or assistance with re-location expenses, these can be included in the advertisement.

Advertisers[10] will also need to be aware of the requirements of the Code of Advertising Practice which sets standards requiring, among other things, decency, honesty and truthfulness; and requires compliance with rules about competitive practices. Although no legal sanctions are involved if there is a breach, the advertiser could find it difficult to obtain advertising space again – a consideration which will be particularly relevant to larger firms which advertise regularly in the media. (See further on discriminatory practices in advertising, pages 43 to 49 below.)

Pay offers/negotiation

Details in a job advertisement, however precise, are unlikely to amount to a formal offer which would then enable a person to conclude a contract by accepting. Except in exceptional cases[11] an advertisement should be regarded as an "invitation to treat", i.e. a request to suitable candidates to start negotiating on the preliminary terms advertised.

The "negotiating" phase begins when an applicant responds to the advertisement. Ideally, this stage should be handled by somebody in the business, such as a personnel officer, who is familiar with:

[10] Employment agencies and businesses are subject to trade description legislation, and are regulated by regulations dealing, among other things, with advertising (see footnote 2 above); Newell, pp. 35, 36.

[11] For example, where it offered *anybody* who satisified specified conditions (e.g. as to experience) specific remuneration if they performed specific tasks – this might amount to an offer to "the world at large" capable of acceptance by an appropriate offeree.

- ☐ the requirements of the post;
- ☐ if it is a new business (or new post), the pay parameters within which the firm has decided to recruit (see pages 34 to 37 above); and
- ☐ if it is an established business, the appropriate pay parameters which are possible within the existing pay structure (see pages 37 to 39 above).

While it may be important to involve other managers and staff in the recruitment process, it is also necessary to ensure that they give correct information on wages conditions – such staff may not always be familiar with pay implications for other employees, the pay structure, etc., of statements or undertakings made to an applicant.

The rules on pay offers can be briefly summarised.[12] To amount to a legally effective offer which is capable of being accepted and forming the basis of a contract, it must be clear and precise – and the *details* of it must normally have been agreed.[13] On the other hand an arrangement for determining pay at a later stage, for example by arbitration, might be offered.[14] Once an offer has been made to the applicant he can accept it at any time until it is withdrawn, or else a reasonable time for accepting it has elapsed.[15] If the applicant *counter-offers* – for example by accepting "if you include a company car" – the effect of this is to *cancel* the firm's offer.

If the salary, benefits, etc., have been agreed on the strength of any special qualifications or experience of

---

[12] For a more detailed description of the rules of "offer and acceptance", see works like Treitel *The Law of Contract* (1987) pp. 7 to 38; and Cheshire, Fifoot and Furmston *Law of Contract* (1986) pp. 26 to 66.

[13] An offer to engage somebody at a West-End salary "to be mutually arranged between us" would not suffice; *Loftus* v *Roberts* XVIII TLR 532 (discussed by Wedderburn p. 133).

[14] *Foley* v *Classique Coaches Ltd.* (1934) 2 K.B. 1.

[15] The offer can specify the way in which it can be accepted. If acceptance is by letter it will be legally effective on posting.

the applicant, then it is possible to make the offer subject to conditions that these are verified (for example in a reference from a previous employer). Sometimes a higher offer is made to match what the applicant has said their previous salary or benefits were – in which case it is obviously worth confirming the details given. Ideally, all offers and counter-offers (including any conditions attaching to them) should be evidenced in written form to avoid arguments later; and when agreement is finally reached on all points these should later be accurately reproduced in the letter of appointment and statement of terms (see page 52 below).

Once the offer has been accepted there will be a binding contract and a failure to implement it will normally give rise to an action for damages. The exact amount may depend on various factors and might only be limited (for example, to the pay due in the period of notice required for ending the contract). The breach of an undertaking or "warranty" to employ at higher wages can be used to establish liability.

☐ *Example*
C.Ltd required insulation engineers, and offered staff who were already working for another company (H.Ltd) higher wages if they would join C.Ltd. On the strength of this promise some employees of H.Ltd left, and were told that they would never be employed by them again. Later, C.Ltd *withdrew* their offer of employment (which they had said would last for six months). It was held that the promise and representations made amounted to a *warranty*. As this had been broken the employees were entitled to damages to compensate them for the employment which had not materialised.[16]

Appointments

After the terms have been settled it is always advisable to confirm the details of the appointment in writing, and

[16] *Gill and others* v *Cape Contracts Ltd.* (1985) IRLR 499.

this should be sent to the appointee well *before* the date of commencement. A letter of appointment will generally be the best evidence of the precise pay terms which have been agreed; and unless there is any later disparity between the letter and any further statement of terms provided, it will avoid the possibility of a request to an industrial tribunal to decide what the appropriate wage terms are (see pages 53 to 54 below).

In the absence of any record of an appointee's acceptance of particular terms (or a letter of appointment) it is, of course, possible to show acceptance or "acquiesence" on the strength of his working to those terms without objecting to them: for example, it might be reasonable to expect him to have queried any point he disagreed with – particularly if it clearly showed on his itemised pay statement – within the first four or five pay days of him starting. It is by no means clear, however, that an industrial tribunal or court will always conclude there *has* been "acceptance" in this way, and so it is not a way of doing things which can be recommended!

3.4 Discriminatory pay offers and practices

In the rest of this chapter attention is given to rules on discrimination over pay matters at the recruitment and commencement stage. These rules are generally applicable to either established or new businesses.

The statutory framework

The Sex Discrimination Act 1975 (SDA) is concerned with discrimination on the grounds of gender and marital status and applies to offers of employment. This area is also covered by the Race Relations Act 1976 (RRA) which deals with discrimination on racial grounds. "Racial grounds" refers to "colour, race, nationality or ethnic or national origins . . ."[17] so it is not limited to

[17] RRA s.3.

race in just the biological sense.[18] It is possible for both men and white persons to be discriminated against under the respective Acts although examples below will assume women and black persons to be the main potential claimants.

Employment agencies and other organisations in the employment field can be liable,[19] as can independent contractors on contracts to personally execute any work (e.g. a householder employing a local plumber).

Before proceeding, reference must be made to the Equal Pay Act 1970 (EPA) which is concerned with differences in terms and conditions of employment between the sexes after an offer of employment has been accepted. This is because a claim for sex discrimination concerning the terms offered a woman *which relate to the payment of money* (i.e. wage levels) will fail unless it would have succeeded under the EPA if the offer had been accepted.[20] Therefore a woman must look to the provisions of the EPA as well as the SDA before bringing a claim for discrimination in the wages offered by an employer. The EPA is dealt with in Chapter 6 below. It operates in a very different way from the SDA, and a number of classes of people who would succeed in a SDA claim would *not* do so in an EPA one. To give one clear example, there is no reference in the EPA to unequal treatment of married persons. So someone discriminated against on these grounds in the matter of wages offered is effectively barred from succeeding in a claim against an employer. This restriction does not apply to racial discrimination where the RRA has its own provisions relating to discrimination in employment terms during the course of employment.[21]

---

[18] See *Mandla* v *Lee* (1983) IRLR 209, H.L.
[19] See SDA ss.11 to 16 and RRA ss.10 to 15.
[20] SDA s.6(5) and s.8(4).
[21] See page 121 below.

Discrimination in wages offered

SDA section 6(1), RRA section 4(1):

> "It is unlawful for a person, in relation to employment by him at an establishment in Great Britain, to discriminate against a woman (another) . . .
> . . .(b) in the terms on which he offers her (him) that employment . . ."

The Acts recognise two types of discrimination:

(a) *Direct discrimination* is where the employer on the grounds of gender or race treats a person less favourably than he would treat a person of the opposite sex or someone not of the same racial group.[22]

☐ *Example*
An employer has two vacancies for identical posts. He offers one to a white person at a salary of £10,000 per annum and one to a black person at a salary of £9500 per annum because he believes white people "work harder".

(b) *Indirect discrimination* is more commonly the subject of a claim. An employer will indirectly discriminate where he applies to a woman (or black person) . . .

> "a requirement or condition which applies or would apply equally to a man (a white person) but
>
> i) which is such that the proportion of women (black persons) who can comply with it is considerably smaller than the proportion of men (white persons) who can comply with it . . ."[23]

In addition an applicant must show detriment to herself (himself) arising from the employer's actions.

☐ *Example*
An employer has 20 identical posts to fill but decides

---

[22] SDA and RRA s.1(1)(a).
[23] SDA and RRA s.1(1)(b).

to pay those successful applicants who are aged 40 or over a lesser salary than the others. This, on the face of it, is an example of indirect discrimination (there being no such legal concept as age discrimination it cannot be direct). This is because the requirement of being under 40 to qualify for the higher salary is likely to proportionately affect far more women who tend to have child caring responsibilities at that stage in their lives.

It has been assumed that the "pool" of women used in the above example for comparison is the female population as a *whole* who are qualified for a post and not a narrower sample such as those women who actually *applied for a post*. This has generally been the view taken by the Tribunals in hearing these types of claims, and, is likely to be followed by the higher courts.[24] The words "can comply", in the statutes have also been interpreted liberally to mean can *practicably* comply, so that, to use the above example, although it may be actually *possible* to arrange child care by neighbours, relations or social services in cases of necessity, it is not *practicable* for most women.

Defences

Mention has already been made of the role of the EPA in frustrating a sex discrimination claim.[25] In addition, because the Acts state that discrimination must be "on the grounds of" gender or race an employer can argue that his actions were made on completely *different* grounds.

☐ *Example*
In the previous example given in para. 3. the employer may be able to show that it was because all the applicants of 40 or over were *less well qualified* that he offered them less, their age being immaterial.

[24] *Pearse* v *City of Bradford Metropolitan Council* (1988) IRLR 379.
[25] See page 44 above.

'Justification' This is a statutory defence only available in claims for indirect discrimination where the employer shows his actions to be;

" . . . justifiable irrespective of the sex (race etc.) of the person to whom it is applied . . ."[26]

There must have been a reason not related to the sex or race of the applicant for treating that applicant in a discriminatory manner and the test is that the discrimination be at least for "sound and tolerable" reasons.[27] However, it seems for women who are government employees (or of other "quasi state organisations") EEC law must prevail and this says the employer can only justify his actions by proving that they were for *necessary* reasons.[28]

☐ *Example*
Again using the example in para. 3. The employer may be able to show that national statistics in his industry reveal that employees aged under 40 are more productive than the others and therefore justify the pay differential. This, if proven, may well satisfy the "sound and tolerable" reason test.

Employers' liability

An employer is liable for the discriminatory acts of his employees (such as personnel officers, managers etc.), but there is a defence if he can prove that he took "such steps as were reasonably practicable to prevent the employee from doing that act . . ."[29]

---

[26] SDA and RRA s.1(1)(b)(ii).
[27] *Ojutiku and Oburoni* v *Manpower Services Commission* (1982) IRLR 418, C.A.
[28] See commentary of M. Rubinstein; *Highlights* (1988) IRLR 81 to 82.
[29] SDA s.41(3) and RRA s.32(3).

Remedies

(a) *Procedure* An applicant must apply to an Industrial Tribunal within three months of the act of discrimination complained of, although the Tribunal may extend the time period if it thinks it "just and equitable".[30] At the Tribunal the applicant has to first establish the basis of a claim and then it is for the employer to satisfy the Tribunal that on the balance of the evidence the claim should not succeed.

(b) *Orders* If the claim is successful the Tribunal may make any of the following orders:

☐ a declaration of the party's rights;

☐ an order for money compensation (up to a limit, at present, of £8500); and

☐ a recommendation of steps to be taken by the employer to obviate or reduce the effects of discrimination on the applicant.

A compensation order is assessed in the same manner as damages in an ordinary civil action (i.e. by trying to place the applicant in the same financial position she/he would have been but for the discrimination). Additional compensation can be ordered (up to the statutory limit) if an employer does not carry out a Tribunal's recommendations.[31] There is a right of appeal, on a point of law only, to the Employment Appeal Tribunal and, from there, to the Court of Appeal; and, in exceptional cases to the House of Lords. In addition, the Equal Opportunities Commission (EOC) and the Commission for Racial Equality (CRE), the bodies set up by the respective statutes, have certain powers to initiate investigations and issue legally enforceable "non-discrimination notices".[32]

---

[30] SDA s.76 and RRA s.68.
[31] See SDA s.65 and RRA s.56 on compensation.
[32] SDA s.67 and RRA s.58.

Discriminatory advertisements

It is unlawful to publish or cause to be published an advertisement which indicates, or might reasonably be understood as indicating an intention, by a person to do any act which might be unlawful within the terms of the statutes (i.e. to advertise jobs with different salary levels for men and women (white and black persons)).[33] However, there is a defence for innocent publishers (e.g. newspapers).[34] The provisions are only enforceable by the EOC and CRE.

---

[33] SDA s.38 and RRA s.29.
[34] SDA s.38(4) and RRA s.29(4).

Chapter 4

WAGES: CONTRACT TERMS AND CONDITIONS

4.1 General points

When staff are recruited it is obviously desirable to try to ensure that all wages matters are clearly identified and understood from the outset, so ideally, important details should be available in a single, comprehensive document. In practice, though, wages terms (and supplementary points and procedures, etc. related to them) are introduced into "the contract" by a variety of *other* avenues than just the "offer and acceptance" process that takes place on recruitment and which was discussed in the last chapter.

It is also important to appreciate that the contract of a new member of staff (whether in a new or an established business) is going to *change*. Pay conditions – whether they deal with levels of pay and method of computation, or ancillary matters like intervals of payment, deductions, etc., are the conditions which are most susceptible to regular changes or different interpretation. Although it might be expected that such important alterations should only ever be effected by written agreement with the individual concerned this is *not* necessarily the case. Indeed, the worker (or even perhaps his employer!) might never be aware of an important pay term or change – for example, where such a term is established in an industry-wide customary practice (as in the example in page 60 below); or where a new national collective agreement has improved the terms of a firm's workers, because those terms are subject to automatic revision when the new agreement comes into force (see "Reference to other documents", page 54 below).

The more subtle device for introducing what are *in*

effect pay terms (which is considered further in Chapter 6) – namely through the "reinterpretation" of existing terms, followed by tacit acquiescence or "acceptance" by the other side – is yet another aspect of the way in which new pay conditions can come into being. It also illustrates further how employment contracts are rarely static but will always be subject to any "shifting sands" affecting the employment itself.

In this chapter it is proposed to examine the principal ways in which pay terms can be established in the contract between a firm and its staff; and how, in certain circumstances they may be illegal or ineffective. In addition, the important statutory rules requiring an employer to provide its employees with written statements of terms (and their rights to challenge them in a tribunal) are dealt with. Although it is not essential for would-be employers to become experts on these matters, their importance does in practical terms require familiarity with the "basics".

4.2 Source of pay terms

Pay terms can be introduced into the contract in four main ways. They may be:

☐ *expressly* agreed with the employer (either by the individual or his union in a collective agreement);

☐ *implied*;

☐ contained in *rules, notices, etc.*; and

☐ established by *custom and practice*.

Each of these sources are considered in turn, particularly as they relate to wages points.

4.3 Express Terms

The employer and employee can agree to terms and conditions in a written contract – that is to say a written

51

document which they intend should have binding consequences. More frequently, though, conditions are merely *evidenced* by written documents, for example, a letter of engagement, or memos and letters sent after the job has begun.

Statement of terms

There is, in any case, a statutory requirement to provide most employees – the main exception being employees working less than sixteen hours a week (unless they can show they have worked eight to sixteen hours a week for five years) – with a *written statement* of the main terms and conditions of the contract.[1] This must be done within thirteen weeks of commencement. The statement must relate to a specified date not more than a week before it is issued.

As far as wages are concerned the most important requirements are that it shows:

☐ the *scale or rate* or remuneration, or the method of calculating it;

☐ the *intervals* at which payment is made (i.e. whether weekly, monthly, or at some other interval).

☐ *hours* of work (including any terms about normal working hours); and

☐ *sickness, injury, holiday pay,* and details about *pension schemes.*

The requirements are satisfied if employees are referred to documents to which they have reasonable access, and have a reasonable opportunity of reading them. If changes in terms are agreed these must be notified within a month of the change.

The statement can in some cases be regarded as a

---

[1] EPCA Part I (ss.1 to 11); for further guidance, see *Written Statement of Main Terms and Conditions of Employment* (Dept. of Employment PL700).

written contract *in itself*. This will be where the employee signs it, not just as a receipt, but as acknowledgement that it is, in itself, a binding contract.[2] Otherwise the statement is merely strong *evidence* of what the contract terms are, and normally represents just a unilateral expression by the employer of his *view* of those terms[3] – something which can be challenged in a tribunal court.

☐ *Example*
R. was told in his letter of appointment that he would receive an incentive bonus. He also got a statement of terms saying that any bonus payments which might be due would be calculated in accordance with the rules of the scheme "in force at that time". When the employer terminated the scheme no further bonus was paid. In these circumstances it was open to R. to argue that the *letter* set out the correct contractual position, and that he was entitled to go on receiving payments.[4]

Non-compliance

If details about pay have not been properly (or correctly) notified an employee can ask an industrial tribunal to decide what the statement *ought* to have contained.[5] The main powers of the tribunal are[6] to:

☐ confirm the particulars as they have been provided;

☐ amend those particulars; and

☐ substitute other particulars for them as it considers appropriate.

[2] *Gascol Conversions Ltd.* v *J. W. Mercer* (1974) IRLR 155 at 156 to 157.
[3] *System Floors (UK) Ltd.* v *Daniel* (1981) IRLR 475 at 476 to 477.
[4] *Robertson* v *British Gas Corporation* (1983) ICR 351.
[5] EPCA s.11: see *Mears* v *Safecar Security Ltd.*, (1982) 3 WLR, 366, C.A. on the tribunal's powers under s.11.
[6] EPCA s.11(6).

The statement, if adjusted by the tribunal, is then *deemed* to have been given by the employer to the employee. In deciding an application the tribunal will look at all the relevant circumstances, including what was said at the time of engagement, and what has happened since that time.

Changes in terms

These must be notified within one month of the change being made[7] (see further page 114 below).

Reference to other documents

It is quite common, and legally permissible, to *refer* the new employee to a document which expressly sets out wage conditions. Thus a letter of appointment may state that the employment is on the same terms and conditions as the local authority's published working conditions (see, for example, *Cadoux* v *Central Regional Council*, page 112 below); or in a *collective agreement* negotiated between employer and a union. The letter may also make it clear that the individual's terms and conditions can automatically *change* should the document, collective agreement, etc., be changed – for example by referring in the letter to such collective agreements as may "from time to time" be negotiated or revised.

This process is known as "incorporation by reference", and it has been described as providing a "bridge", between documents like collective agreements and the individual's contract. Once that bridge has been crossed, i.e. a term has been incorporated into the individual contract, that term will give him legally-enforceable rights. Thus, in the case of *Robertson* v *British Gas Corporation* already referred to[8] a collective

---

[7] EPCA s.4.
[8] *Robertson* v *British Gas Corporation*, see footnote 4 above.

agreement had established the bonus scheme under which R. received payments. But while the employer could unilaterally terminate the *collective* agreement by giving notice to the union,[9] the employee's entitlement to bonus *continued*. It was stated in the Court of Appeal that:[10]

> "It is true that collective agreements such as those in the present case create no legally enforceable obligation between the trade union and the employers. Either side can withdraw. But their terms are in this case incorporated into the individual contracts of employment, and it is only if and when those terms are varied collectively by agreement that the individual contracts of employment will also be varied. If the collective scheme is not varied by agreement, but by some unilateral abrogation or withdrawal or variation to which the other side does not agree, then it seems to me that the individual contracts of employment remain unaffected. This is another way of saying that the terms of the individual contracts are in part to be found in the agreed collective agreements as they exist from time to time, and, if these cease to exist as collective agreements, then the terms, unless expressly varied between the individual and the employer, will remain as they were by reference to the last agreed collective agreement incorporated into the individual contracts."

4.4 Implied terms

If a point has not been dealt with in writing, or there is no evidence to suggest oral agreement, it may be possible to *imply* agreement. Indeed it has been said that a

---

[9] Note collective agreements are not, in themselves, legally binding unless the parties state that they *should* be; TULRA s.18; *NCB* v *NUM* (1986) IRLR 439 at 449.

[10] (1983) ICR 351 at 358.

contract of employment cannot simply be treated as "silent" on important matters like pay or the place of work – in which case it may be essential to imply a term to *make* the contract workable.[11] In practice, tribunals and courts readily imply wages and other terms into employment contracts unless to do so would contradict expressly–agreed terms which are clear and unambiguous.[12]

In relation to wages issues implied terms can be invoked to deal with relatively minor matters, or be used even to establish a right to wages in the first place. Thus, even where it is impossible to say how the parties would have completed their contract, it may be possible to imply:

(a) a basic right to reasonable remuneration; and then

(b) what that remuneration is to *consist* of:

□ *Example*
A. claimed that he had an agreement with B. that, in return for information and work in acquiring mining concessions, he would be paid a reasonable sum. It was held that the arrangement amounted to a contract of employment, and indicated that the work was not gratuitously done. On the evidence there was an implied right to be paid a suitable amount for participation in the venture, and this would consist of a share in profits as well as a basic fee.[13]

A general test for deciding whether to imply a term in a contract is to ask whether such a term is necessary in order to give efficacy to the parties' agreement, in a way that those parties would have intended.[14] Adopting this

---

[11] *Jones* v *Associated Tunnelling Co. Ltd.*, (1981) IRLR 477 at 480.

[12] *Ibid* at p.481. So express provision in a company's articles of association dealing with directors' pay will remove any inference that a director should be paid for work done; *In Re Richmond Gate Property Ltd.* (1965) 1 WLR 335.

[13] *Way* v *Latilla* (1937) 3 All E.R. 759.

[14] *The Moorcock* (1889) 14 PD 64. More recently it has been said

approach, the tribunal or court accepts the term on the basis that it was one which both parties would have immediately agreed was necessary had they been asked at the time the contract was made. An alternative approach (and the one now frequently used) was suggested in a case concerned with sick pay.[15] This is that where a term is required but it is unlikely that the parties would have agreed on one, it is up to the court to imply a term which it considers *reasonable*.

In the above case the Employment Appeal Tribunal accepted that an obligation to pay sick pay had been established, but there was no agreed term as to the *duration* it was to be paid. Rather than apply a presumption that it had to be paid until the employment terminated, it was decided that a reasonable term should be implied that the payment should only be for a *limited* period. It based this, among other things, on what was the norm in the industry concerned and what "industrial relations common sense" required.

In practice, tribunals have regard to a wide range of matters before deciding whether wages terms can be implied. They may be inferred, for example, from the custom or practice in the industry; from the type of contract concerned; and from whether payments of the kind in issue have been claimed by the employee, or paid, on previous occasions.[16]

Although there may be situations in which terms are easily implied, cases turn on their own particular facts and evidence rather than on any generalised presumptions. There is not, therefore, a general implied term that employees are *entitled* to an annual pay rise. Thus, while there may be a term inferred that the employer must not

---

that it must be shown that the term is necessary, the contract would make no sense without it, and that it was omitted from negotiations because it was so obvious that there was no need to make it explicit; *Stubbs* v *Trower, Still & Keeling* (1987) IRLR 321, C.A.

[15] *Howman & Son* v *Blyth* (1983) ICR 416.
[16] *Mears* see footnote 5 above.

act unfairly in not paying rises to staff,[17] in other cases it may be unjustified to impose any particular requirements, or to imply a right to an annual increase.

☐ *Example*
F. resigned from her job after more than ten years because she had not received a salary increase, and after being told that this was because her work was not up to standard. She was the only employee not to receive a rise. The tribunal held that her claim for constructive dismissal must succeed as the employer had broken an implied term that she should have such an increase. This was evidenced by, among other things, the fact that she had received a rise in previous years. This was reversed, though, on appeal. To imply such a term was not, on the facts of the case, considered reasonable. An implied right to an annual rise was not established in industry. The correct approach, which had not been taken by the tribunal, was to ask whether the employer had acted arbitrarily or capriciously so as to have broken the duty of mutual trust and confidence owed between the parties.[18]

4.5 Rules and notices

Workplace rules and notices can have an important bearing on wages and the way in which they are paid. They might, for example, be evidence of the existence of a right to make deductions for disciplinary offences, or possibly lay down conditions for the payment, for example, of overtime or sickness payments. As employers frequently use notice-boards, "rule-books", etc., to communicate information and instructions it is important to consider how these might be effective in establishing contractual conditions.

[17] *F.C. Gardner Ltd* v *Beresford* (1978) IRLR 63.
[18] *Murco Petroleum Ltd.* v *Forge* (1987) IRLR 50.

In principle wages entitlements cannot be determined by the employer simply and *unilaterally* stating what that entitlement is to be, or purporting to make alterations to it (see, further, Chapter 6 below on changes to wages). The only circumstances in which rules and notices can be used in this way are where:

☐ the individual contract of employment specifically authorises this;[19] or

☐ there is an agreement to do so (for example with a union representing the staff concerned).

There may be situations in which a notice deals with rights to such matters as sick pay, and, because its contents are *so* well known *and* accepted by staff, they can be said to be "contractual", and therefore legally govern the payment of the wages.[20] Apart from this possibility, works rules and notices should generally be regarded as simply managerial instructions or guidance.[21]

In some circumstances a works rule-book can be invoked by the employer to clarify, or confirm the existence of a contractual term which is evidenced in other ways. Thus, if an employee's statement of terms states that wages may vary according to the particular job being undertaken, a statement in the rule-book that the management can transfer him between jobs and vary the pay is supporting evidence, at the least, that the employer has a contractual right to do this. If the rule-book is incorporated into the contract (i.e. by referring to it as a source of terms) then the rule *itself* may have contractual force.

---

[19] See *Cadoux* v *Central Regional Council* (1986). IRLR 131 (page 112 below).

[20] See, for example, *Petrie* v *MacFisheries Ltd.*, (1940) 1 K.B. 258 (1939) 4 All E.R. 281.

[21] See *Secretary of State for Employment* v *ASLEF and others (No.2)* (1972) 2 All E.R. 949; *Automotive Products Ltd.*v *F. B. Peake*, (1977) IRLR 365; and see, further Smith and Wood pp.144, 145.

4.6 Custom and practice

Wages terms may be established on the strength of custom and practice, either in the industry or area concerned or, possibly, on the basis of the practice in a particular workplace.

☐ *Example*
S. was a weaver whose pay had been docked for bad workmanship. There was evidence that this form of action had been the practice for at least thirty years at the mill; and furthermore that the practice was well-established in the Lancashire cotton trade. Even if S. had not been aware of this when he started the job, the fact that he accepted employment on the same terms as to deductions as the other weavers was regarded as sufficient to enable the employer to incorporate the right to make deductions into his contract.[22]

There is some doubt, however, as to whether the employee must actually know or be told of the custom and practice before it can form part of his contract. It would seem the term might be established simply on the basis that it is so universally known that the worker could not be supposed to have started the job without regarding it as part of the contract.[23] On the other hand it has been held that a term *cannot* be annexed to the contract if the employee is, in fact, unaware of it when he started the employment.

☐ *Example*
Port employees were promoted, and the employers thereupon stopped paying income tax on their pay (something which had been the practice with other staff). The court refused to treat the practice as a contractual term. Even if the practice had existed for a

---

[22] *Sagar* v *H. Ridehalgh & Son Ltd.*, (1930) All E.R. 288, 297.
[23] *R.* v *Inhabitants of Stoke-upon-Trent* (1843) 5 Q.B. 303; *Devonald* v *Rosser & Sons* (1906) 2 K.B. 728, 733, 741.

long time, and was universally established, the employees had no knowledge of the practice when they started, and they were not referred to it at that time. *Prima facie* such practices should be regarded as a "bounty" by the employer rather than as something capable of becoming a contractual obligation.[24]

As a general rule it is difficult to establish wages terms on the basis of custom and practice unless their existence is clearly confirmed by consistent application in previous cases. But even this may not necessarily be enough. Thus in the shipbuilding industry the fact that supervisors had, in the past, lost a chargehand's allowance after being demoted did not automatically establish this as a management right.

☐ *Example*
S. was paid a £4 additional allowance after being promoted to a "chargeman" grade. Later he was demoted and the allowance was withdrawn. This was held to be a repudiation of the contract, and the demotion and withdrawal of the allowance was not justified by any established custom and practice. The fact that in the past this had been done with the *agreement* of the chargemen concerned was not enough to establish this as a managerial *right* in later cases.[25]

4.7 Validity and enforcement of wages terms

Rules of contract

Employment contracts are subject to the general rules of contract with regard to their validity and enforceability. A detailed discussion is outside the scope of this book.[26]

---

[24] *Meek* v *Port of London Authority* (1918) 1 Ch.415.
[25] *F.G. Samways* v *Swan Hunter Shipbuilders Ltd.*, (1975) IRLR 190; see also *Bond* v *CAV Ltd.*, p. 88 below.
[26] See Cheshire, Fifoot and Furmston's *Law of Contract* (1986), 11th edn); Treitel *Law of Contract* (1987, 7th edn).

The most important of these, as far as wages terms are concerned, include the requirement or *certainty* as to what those terms are.[27] A *mistake*, or *misunderstanding*, as to what the wages terms are might also make a contract inoperative. In the employment field *illegality* of the contract, or in the way it is performed, is in practical terms particularly important.

Statutory restrictions

An Act or legislative instrument can impose express or implied prohibitions on the making of contracts, and in this event the courts may not enforce them.

☐ *Example*
C. worked for R. by buying and disposing of stocks and shares. He did not, however, have a licence to do so as required by Statute, and which also made him liable to penalty. A legal action to have his fees paid failed on the ground that contracts for such work had to be taken as prohibited by law.[28]

Contracts to defraud government bodies like the Inland Revenue are illegal and it is not possible, therefore, to rely on them in the courts or tribunals, for example when suing for arrears of wages due.

☐ *Example*
N. was employed at a salary of £13 per week with £6 a week "expenses". In fact his expenses never exceeded £1 a week. After he was summarily dismissed he sued for wages in lieu of notice. It was held that he could not recover either the expenses *or*, even, his basic salary. The whole contract was illegal, and he was unable to argue that there was a "legal" part which could be severed from the rest.[29]

---

[27] See Ch. 3 above and footnote 12 thereto: and see, further, Wedderburn p.133.
[28] *Cope* v *Rowlands* (1836) 2 M & W 149.
[29] *Napier* v *National Business Agency Ltd.*, (1951) 2 All E.R. 264;

In cases where the contract is *illegal from the outset* (for example where it is barred by Statute it is irrelevant whether the parties were aware of the illegality or not. However, where the illegality lies in the *performance* of the contract, a party who is not involved in the illegality, and is unaware of it, can still rely on the contract (and therefore bring complaints of unfair dismissal, sue for wages dues, etc.).

□ *Example*

N. was paid a weekly wage in cash. She was dismissed and brought a claim for unfair dismissal. It then came to light that the employers had entered lower amounts in their wages records than had, in fact, been paid to her in order to defraud the Revenue. Initially, N. was unaware of this fact, although the tribunal concluded that she later became aware (or ought to have realised) that tax was not being properly paid. The tribunal therefore dismissed her claim. On appeal the EAT held that although the contract was not necessarily illegal (payment of wages free of tax not, in itself, producing this result), the illegal *performance* of it rendered it unenforceable as far as the *employer* was concerned. Whether the *employee* was precluded from relying on the contract (to pursue her claim) depended, though, on whether she knew of the employer's illegal activities. The case was remitted to the industrial tribunal to consider this aspect further.[30]

Employers that are public bodies

The actions of public bodies, such as local authorities, must be carried out within their statutory or other

---

applied in *F.H.C. Cole* v *Fred Stacey Ltd.*, (1974) IRLR 73 (part of weekly wage paid under the guise of expenses and Sunday working paid out of petty cash and not declared for tax: redundancy payment not payable).
[30] *Newland* v *Simons & Willer (Hairdressers) Ltd.*, (1981) ICR 521; and see also *McConnell* v *Bolik* (1979) IRLR 422.

powers. If they are not they are liable to challenge in the courts. As far as wages are concerned payments must, if they are not to be challenged in the courts or by an auditor,[31] be authorised by law and ought to be fixed at the correct level by reference to such factors as market rates for the job, what other public bodies pay etc..

In the leading case of *Roberts* v *Hopwood and others*[32] it was held that wages paid to council staff were illegal to the extent that they exceeded what was the "going rate" for workers doing the work concerned. However, in the later case of *Pickwell* v *Camden LBC*[33] the court considered that to establish such illegality would require it to be shown that the council had *acted unreasonably* (for example for some ulterior motive), or in a way that no reasonable council would have done. In this case, making a local settlement with its striking workers at pay levels that were higher than a later nationally-agreed settlement (and including a reduction in the working week to thirty-five hours) was not treated as beyond the council's powers.

Government policies

At different times in the past, statutory and administrative controls over wages and wage increases have been a major feature of the pay scene. The use of statutory powers reached a high-point in the early 1970s with the Pay Board, and powers to control increases in accordance with a statutory code. This legislation produced important cases on wages issues which may become relevant if statutory pay controls are reintroduced.

The first important case demonstrates that the courts will, where possible, apply legislation regulating pay in favour of preserving employees' contractual rights.

---

[31] Local Government Finance Act 1982, s.19.
[32] (1925) A.C. 578.
[33] (1983) 1 Q.B. 962; and, see further on local authority expenditure and audit, Cross on *Local Government Law* (1986), Ch.7.

☐ *Example*
S. was a sales assistant who was awarded a pay increase from 31 December, 1972 under a collective agreement made on 8 May, 1972 (and due to be paid from 31 December, 1972). The employers refused to pay the increase, claiming this would be in breach of the pay controls. The court concluded that the legislation could be interpreted either the employee's way, on the basis that it only applied to wages earned *after* an order implementing the controls came into effect (on 5 February, 1973); *or* in favour of the employers on the basis that the restrictions could be construed as operating *before* that date. In this situation it was held that an interpretation which interfered with the employee's rights as little as possible should be adopted. The increase *would* therefore be paid to her for the weeks prior to the order coming into force.[34]

In other leading cases[35] it has been made clear that claims for unfair dismissal based on non-payment of wages or increases will not succeed where to do so may breach statutory pay controls. In one case it was even said that if the employer misinterpreted the legislation and *mistakenly* refused to pay wages due, this would *not* necessarily amount to repudiatory breach of the contract that could entitle the employee to claim unfair dismissal.

In relation to *non*-statutory pay policies it would probably be harder for an employer to rely on such policies to justify a failure to pay wages due to an employee under a contract. But even here the tribunals have been prepared to take into account the difficulties employers are faced with in not implementing a government pay policy when it comes to deciding the fairness of a dismissal (see *Gillon* page 117 below).

[34] *D.G. Summerfield* v *London Co-operative Society Ltd.*, (1973) ICR 568; IRLR 230, cty. court.
[35] *C.S. Mackay* v *Peter Pan Playthings Ltd.*, (1973) IRLR 232; and see Smith and Wood pp.413 to 415. See also *Industrial Rubber Products* v *C. Gillon* (1977) IRLR 389, discussed in page 117 below.

Chapter 5

RESPONSIBILITIES DURING THE CONTRACT

In this chapter we can look at the basic responsibility of the employer to pay wages in accordance with the contract, and the situations in which that may be affected. In doing so, the requirements of employment legislation must also be considered. Reference will also be made to the main responsibilities assumed by the state for wage earners, through social security payments which supplement their earnings.

5.1 Requirement to pay wages

Once the employee has been appointed the employer's legal obligation to pay wages – at the *rate*, *interval*, and *manner* agreed in the contract – will normally continue until the employee leaves. There may, however, be exceptional situations (for example during industrial action or lay-off) in which this obligation ends, or the level of wages payable will be different. These possibilities are discussed later in this chapter.

Itemised pay statement

An important obligation on employers is to ensure that their employees should receive,[1] at or before the time wages are paid, a written statement showing:

☐ the *gross amount* of wages or salary;

---

[1] EPCA s.8. See, further, Dept. of Employment Guidance *Itemised Pay Statement* (PL 704).

- ☐ the amount of any *variable deductions* made, and, subject to exceptions (noted below), any *fixed deductions* from that amount, and the purpose for which they are made;

- ☐ the *net amount* of wages or salary payable; and

- ☐ where different parts of the net amount are paid in different ways, *the amount and method of payment of each part-payment.*

A variable deduction must always be explained in the pay statement: and it cannot just be included under "miscellaneous deduction payment" or some other label.

- ☐ *Example*
  M. was given £111.68 by his employers to cover the costs of a course he was taking. When he left he was asked to repay this sum. He disputed their right to do this. Later it was deducted from his pay, and in the column of his pay-slip specifying the nature of the deduction the code "No. 70" appeared. On the back of the slip this simply said "Miscellaneous deduction/payment". It was held that this did not give sufficient information about the *purposes* of the deduction.[2]

Fixed deductions

These include deductions authorised by legislation (for example maintenance payments), or under the contract (for example union dues). Instead of having to provide details of every fixed deduction made on each pay occasion, the *aggregate* amount of such deductions made may suffice in a pay statement. This is where a "standing statement" of deductions has been provided.[3] It must contain the following particulars about each deduction comprised in the aggregate amount:

- ☐ the amount of the deduction;

[2] *Milsom* v *Leicestershire County Council* (1978) IRLR 433.
[3] EPCA s.9.

☐ the intervals at which it is to be made; and

☐ its purpose.

Changes to the statement must be notified to the employee in writing. Standing statements are effective for a maximum of twelve months from being issued. If they are to continue they must be re-issued, incorporating any amendments made in the preceding period.

Remedies for non-compliance

If an itemised pay statement is not provided, or is incomplete or inaccurate, application may be made (normally within a three month period) to an industrial tribunal.[4] If the complaint is well-founded the tribunal must make a declaration of what should have been included in the statement. It can also order the employer to pay the employee a sum of up to the equivalent of all the unnotified deductions made in the thirteen weeks prior to the application.

An important point to note is that this can be done whether the deductions were in breach of contract or not.

Authority to deduct

Reference should be made to Chapter 7 where the question of authority to deduct is considered. The right to have deductions explained in itemised statements is continued after the Wages Act 1986, even where employees may have given their prior consent to deductions (in the contract or by written authority) in accordance with s.1 of the Act.

Failure to pay wages; delays

If there is a failure to pay wages when they are due this will be a breach of contract, and the employee will be

[4] EPCA s.11. See also p. 20, note 37 above.

able to sue for any amounts due.[5] If there has been a delay in paying wages there might also be circumstances in which the employee may be entitled to resign and claim unfair or "constructive" dismissal. One such case[6] was where a barmaid did not receive her weekly wages, due for the week ending 28 June until 5 July: and her wages for the week ending 12 July until 7 August. After these delayed payments the tribunal accepted she could fairly maintain a claim. It was also said in that case that paying a cheque which is not honoured by the bank may be conduct entitling an employee to bring a claim.

On the other hand, a delay in paying wages, though strictly speaking a breach of contract (actionable in the county court or High Court), may in other circumstances be treated by a tribunal as *not* being sufficiently serious to justify an unfair dismissal claim.

☐ *Example*

A. was a consultant with a firm of management consultants. His pay depended on income arriving from overseas, and there had been problems when that income arrived late. When on a previous occasion a cheque had not been honoured. There was a delay in paying his April salary and he was asked to wait until 2 May for payment. By the 9 May he had still not been paid, whereupon he filed a complaint of unfair dismissal without telling the company. Despite these delays, the tribunal (and a majority of the Employment Appeal Tribunal) rejected his claim. Although the company's conduct was a breach of contract, it was not regarded as significant enough to entitle A. to regard himself as dismissed. He had not raised objections to the delay on 2 May and the employers had not shown that they no longer intended to be bound by the contract.[7]

---

[5] *R. F. Hill Ltd.* v. *Mooney* (page 111 below); and see footnote 29 below.
[6] *A. Hanlon* v *Allied Breweries (UK) Ltd.* (1975) IRLR 321.
[7] *Adams* v *Charles Zub Associates Ltd.* (1978) IRLR 551.

Level of remuneration

In the majority of cases the basic level of remuneration for the job will be fixed when the employee is appointed, and that flat-rate level will remain *constant* until a new rate is fixed; for example when an increase is awarded, or the rate for the job is renegotiated in a collective agreement. Apart from cases in which staff are paid their basic earnings on piece-rates, by commission, etc., the main reason for any fluctuation in gross earnings will be due to occasional "extras" like overtime pay or "merit" payments (see the cases referred to in pages 21 to 22 above).

There are ways, however, in which the parties to an employment contract can specifically provide in *advance* for changes in the basic level of pay (whether increasing or reducing that level). Indeed, in some situations – notably where there is a high turnover of staff – it may be desirable to build into the pay system an arrangement for regular bonuses, profit-sharing, etc. Another consideration is that the work-load or content of the job may increase so that it is necessary to compensate in advance for that possibility.

In all these cases it will be necessary to correctly interpret and apply the contract or collective agreement in question. A difficulty which is commonly encountered is where the employee claims the criteria for re-valuing, re-grading etc., of the job have been satisfied, but the employer resists the employee's interpretation, either of the facts or of the scope of the agreement.

☐ *Example.*

Mrs. Bridgen was appointed on 1 September, 1980 to grade 1 on the lecturers' scale as laid down by the Burnham national agreement. The work-load involved expanded quickly and she requested upgrading to grade II on the pay scale in the agreement – this was agreed to on 13 May, 1982 but it was to be operative only from 1 January, 1983. She then applied for a further re-grading to Senior Lecturer grade which, she believed, reflected the work she was undertaking. This was refused. She left and claimed unfair dismissal on the basis that the authority had not immediately up-graded her to grade II as soon as the work-load reached the unit total of 75 prescribed in the agreement for grade II posts. The relevant clause, however, stated that " ... where a teacher is *appointed* ... to take charge of adult education work ..." There was not, therefore, in the Court of Appeal's view an automatic right to re-grading at *later* stages in the employment when the work increased.[8]

5.2 Sick pay/injury pay

Most employers do, as a matter of good practice (although this is not *legally* required) operate a company sick pay scheme providing short-term and longer-term benefits. This can be financed entirely by the employer or partly financed by contributions from the staff. Benefits are usually provided in the form of full normal pay or partial pay, and generally consist of "topping up" payments to supplement any state benefits which are payable during periods of short-term illness and disability. Income payments, lump-sum payments and other assistance can be provided for longer-term incapacity, as can pensions if there is enforced early retirement. Permanent health insurance and schemes effected through private medical insurance are becoming more popular with employers (on tax aspects, see page 31 above).

Contractual rights

Contracts and collective agreements usually set out the arrangements which are to operate when the employee is off sick, and deal with rights to sick pay and any conditions on it being paid. If, however, there is *no*

---

[8] *Brigden* v *Lancashire County Council* (1987) IRLR 58.

express provision for sick pay, it may still be possible to *imply* a right to be paid during periods of incapacity. Consideration must be given to any relevant custom and practice in the industry or work-place concerned, and generally to all the circumstances of the case: a right to sick pay must not simply be assumed, for example because of the employer's general obligation to go on paying wages while the contract continues.[9] If it is not clear for *how long* a contractual right to be paid is to last, a period that is reasonable will be implied – if the practice in the industry is that it should only be paid for a limited period, this will be followed.[10]

Payments made under a *contract* on a sick day will count towards reducing the liability to pay an employee under the *statutory* sick pay (SSP) scheme, – and, conversely, any statutory payments made will go towards discharging contractual liability.[11] Contractual terms which try to exclude the right to SSP, or require an employee to pay towards the employer's costs will normally be ineffective.[12]

5.3 Statutory Sick Pay (SSP)

Introductory points

Legislation[12] now requires employers to pay Statutory Sick Pay (SSP) to employees, with the following principal exceptions. Those employees who are:

☐ over state pensionable age when their incapacity begins;

☐ working under contracts of three months or less;

---

[9] *Mears* v *Safecar Security Ltd.* (1982) ICR 626, C.A. is the leading case on implying a right to sick pay.
[10] *Howman & Son* v *Blyth* (1983) ICR 416.
[11] SSHBA, Sch. 2, para. 2.
[12] SSHBA, ss.1 (2), 23A.

- ☐ earning under the lower earnings limit (at present £41 per week);
- ☐ yet to start work under their contract;
- ☐ incapacitated while there is a stoppage of work due to a trade dispute at their place of work (unless the employee can prove he did not participate or have a direct interest in the dispute);
- ☐ pregnant and within the "disqualifying period" (namely their maternity pay or maternity allowance periods); and
- ☐ overseas and outside the EEC when the incapacity begins.

If an employee has a day of incapacity for work, that is to say he is either deemed by regulations to be incapacitated, or he is, in the words of the legislation,

"incapable by reason of some specific disease or bodily or mental disablement of doing work which he can reasonably be expected to do" (under his contract)",

his employer must pay him SSP for that day.[13]

Qualifying conditions

To qualify for SSP three basic conditions must be met:[14]

- ☐ the day in question must form part of a "period of incapacity for work" (PIW) consisting of any period of four or more consecutive days, each of which is a day of incapacity.[15] PIWs which are separated by no more

---

[13] SSHBA, Part 1, as amended; and the SSP (G) Regs. as amended, contain the main provisions. For detailed official guidance, see *Employer's Guide to Statutory Sick Pay* (DHSS 1987, N.I. 227): and see Tolley's *Guide to Statutory Sick Pay* (1986). On the background to the scheme, and commentary, see Smith and Wood, pp. 356 to 359.
[14] SSHBA ss.1 (1), (3).
[15] SSHBA s.2.

than eight weeks are treated as a *single* period. All days of the week (including Saturdays, Sundays and holidays) are included in counting consecutive days;

☐ the day in question must fall within a period which is a "period of entitlement".[16] Basically, this means a period beginning with the PIW, and ending with the first of the following:
(a) the end of the PIW;
(b) the day when the employee's maximum entitlement to SSP is reached;
(c) the end of the employment;
(d) in the case of pregnant employees, the day before she becomes disqualified from SSP;

☐ the day in question must be a "qualifying day".[17] This is something which is agreed between employer and the employee (or otherwise dealt with by regulations), but would normally be those days when he is required to work. There must be at least one qualifying day per week.

Limitations on entitlement[18]

SSP is not paid for the first three days of a period of entitlement. Nor should an employee receive, in any one period and as against any one employer, an aggregate amount of SSP which is more than his maximum entitlement. This is the point at which he reaches or passes an entitlement of 28 times his weekly SSP rate. This is a figure which is updated periodically by regulations, but is currently £36.25 (on weekly earnings between £43.00 and £83.99); and £51.20 (on £84.00 and above). The daily level of SSP is the weekly rate divided by the qualifying days in the week concerned (beginning with Sunday).

---

[16] SSHBA s.3.
[17] SSHBA s.4.
[18] SSHBA s.5. (Rates operative from 10 April 1989.)

Notification of incapacity[19]

An employer is entitled to withhold SSP if he has not been properly notified of the incapacity in accordance with notification procedures. Such procedures should be in line with the regulations on notification, but they are generally something left to employers to organise in consultation with staff. In most systems a "self-certification" scheme operates for periods of up to seven days.

Miscellaneous points

As well as requiring employers to provide written reasons for SSP decisions, the legislation enables a dissatisfied employee to ask a social security Adjudication Officer to rule on disputed cases. Appeal from that decision is possible.

Employers can recover what they have paid out in SSP by making deductions from national insurance contribution payments.[20] The rules must have been properly applied, however, and the legislation requires employers to keep detailed records of SSP payments, which can be "spot-checked" by DSS inspectors.

5.4 Injuries at work

Civil Liability

If an employee is injured at work and suffers loss (including financial loss because of time off or because his longer term ability to earn is affected), he may be able to sue for compensation if the injury was the fault of his employer or another of his employees or contractors. Most employers will be covered by insurance and claims

---

[19] SSHBA s.6; SSP (G) Regs., reg. 7.
[20] SSHBA s.9, and regulations made under it.

will often be settled before they get to court. The duty of care owed to those who are "contractors" rather than "employees" will generally be less, although this will depend on the circumstances of the injury and the extent to which the employer was responsible for the way in which the work was carried out.

Income support, pensions, etc.

The problem in most cases will be to ensure that income is maintained during short-term periods of incapacity, although provision is also available (through employers or the State) for longer periods. Most larger employers have arrangements for assisting employees who are off work with injury as a part of their occupational sickness schemes (see pages 31 to 71 above), and these will set out the conditions for being paid, duration of benefits, etc. In any case, Statutory Sick Pay (SSP) will normally be payable for the first twenty-eight weeks of incapacity. If SSP is not payable a claim may be made to the Department of Social Security for Sickness Benefit, which consists of a basic rate of benefit and an addition for adult dependants, and is payable for up to twenty-eight weeks. It is a contributory benefit, which means claimants must satisfy the requisite N.I. Class 1 contribution conditions (on N.I. contribution deductions see page 146 below). The benefit could still be claimed, though (even if there are insufficient contributions) as long as the injury was caused by an accident arising out of, and in the course of, the employment. Claimants must be incapable of work, and must not undertake other paid employment. After twenty-eight weeks a claim for Invalidity Benefit (consisting of a basic rate of benefit plus extras for adult dependants and children) can be made. This is payable until he is fit to resume work or he retires. If the individual is unable to return to his normal job (or another job with the same pay), any rights to compensation will generally depend on his contractual rights and any arrangements which can be satisfactorily reached with the employer. In any case Reduced Earnings Allowance, Industrial Disablement Benefit, and a relatively new non-contributory entitlement, Severe Disablement Allowance, may be payable. In the case of a worker who is in "full-time" employment – thirty hours a week for a couple, twenty-four hours a week for a single person – and who is on a low income (for whatever reason), Family Credit is available (see *Family Credit* DHSS Guidance FC1).

In the event of death as a result of injury at work, provision may in the first instance be provided under the employer's own arrangements. As far as the State is concerned, Industrial Death Benefit is provided in the form of pensions and allowances for widows and widowers; parents and other dependant relatives; and children (see further DHSS Guidance N.I.10).

For more information on these and other benefits reference should be made to guides like *Injured at Work: A Guide to Cash Benefits* (DHSS FB.15); and works like Tolley's *Social Security and State Benefits* (latest edition).

Taxation of benefits

SSP is liable to both Income Tax and National Insurance deductions as if it were ordinary income. Sickness Benefit, Invalidity Benefit and Severe Disablement Allowance are not generally liable to tax (there are exceptions in the case of certain additions).

Appeals

Claimants and people who may be *affected* by decisions on benefits made by Adjudication Officers, Adjudicating Medical Authorities, etc. (including in some circumstances employers), can usually appeal against those decisions. Guidance is provided in *How to Appeal* (DHSS Guidance N.I. 246 (1988)).

5.5 Pay during medical suspension

Employees have a statutory right to be paid if they are suspended on medical grounds when this is required by legislation or a health and safety code of practice.[21] They must normally have been continuously employed for a month prior to the suspension; and will not be entitled to be paid if offered suitable alternative work which is refused, or if they do not comply with reasonable requirements to ensure availability for work. Payment is for up to a maximum of twenty-six weeks,[22] and any payments made as a result of *contractual* rights will go towards discharging the statutory obligation (and vice-versa).

5.6 Holiday pay

There is no legal requirement to give paid holiday leave, so any rights to this will depend on what is in the employee's conditions of service. Holiday entitlement may exist as a result of an industry or trade custom – but this can be overridden by express terms (in the employee's contract or in a collective agreement). Public holidays – notably Good Friday and Christmas Day (or the next working day in lieu of those days if they fall on the week-end) are customarily given as paid leave, but there is no general legal requirement to do so.

The Banking and Financial Dealings Act 1971, Schedule 1, states that certain days are to be Bank Holidays. Although it is customary to give these as holiday days, there is no legal requirement to do so, or to pay for them if they are given.

A complication which can arise is where managements try to reorganise agreed arrangements for taking paid holiday.

[21] EPCA ss.19 to 22.
[22] For calculation, see EPCA s.21 and Sch. 14.

☐ *Example*
T. objected to an arrangement whereby the August Bank holiday and New Year's holiday were "transferred" so that those days were to be used instead to give a week off between Monday 27 December and Friday 31 December. T. was given an assurance that the transfer would only be made if all the unions in their plant agreed. Later the Works Committee (but not all the unions) agreed the change. It was held that the management had no power to transfer holiday entitlement without T's consent, or after an agreement which had been properly reached with the unions.[23]

If flexibility is required by an employer over when leave is taken, a clause dealing with this can, of course, be included in the terms of new staff or negotiated in collective agreements. In order to obtain agreement to introduce such flexibility into existing arrangements it may be necessary to offer improved holiday pay terms.

Certain protective legislation (notably the Factories Act 1961) requires women and young persons to be given paid holiday on Bank Holidays, and on Good Friday and Christmas Day. Wages councils' orders can no longer stipulate paid holiday days, since the Wages Act 1986.

5.7 Statutory Maternity Pay

Women employees who can satisfy certain qualifying conditions can claim the following statutory rights:

☐ protection from dismissal by reason of pregnancy;[24]

☐ paid time-off to receive ante-natal care;[25]

---

[23] *Tucker and others* v British Leyland Motor Corporation Ltd. (1978) IRLR 493.
[24] EPCA s.60 (1).
[25] EPCA s.31 (A).

- the right to return to work following confinement;[26] and

- Maternity Pay.[27]

In this section, we examine Statutory Maternity Pay (SMP).

The SMP scheme came into effect on 6 April 1987. Women who are not entitled to SMP are able to claim the State Maternity Allowance.

Qualifying conditions

- Only "employees" are entitled to SMP. A wholly self-employed woman[28] is, therefore, outside the scheme.

- The woman must have been employed by her employer for a continuous period of at least twenty-six weeks ending with the qualifying week, i.e. the fifteenth week before "expected week of confinement" (EWC).

- Her "normal weekly earnings" must be not less than the lower earnings contribution in force at the time (£41 from 6 April 1988).

- She must still be pregnant, or have already been confined, at the commencement of the eleventh week before the EWC.

- She must give her employer twenty-one days' notice of her absence or, if that is not reasonably practicable, such notice as is reasonably practicable. The employer may request the notice to be given in writing.

- She must provide her employer with evidence as to her pregnancy. The evidence must normally be sub-

[26] EPCA s.45.
[27] See the Social Security Act, 1986 and the Statutory Maternity Pay (General) Regulations 1986 (SI No 1960). For detailed guidance, see *Maternity Benefits: A Technical Guide* (N.I. 17A DHSS 1987); and Marsh Ch.18.
[28] See pp. 6 to 8 above.

mitted not later than the end of the third week after the date that SMP was due to start. If she has "good cause", the evidence may be submitted later, but not later than the thirteenth week of the maternity pay period. The evidence will normally take the form of a medical certificate (form Mat B1) which is supplied by the doctor or midwife no earlier than fourteen weeks before the baby is due.

The maternity pay period

SMP is payable for each week during the "maternity pay period" for a maximum of eighteen consecutive weeks, normally commencing with the eleventh week before and ending with the sixth week after the EWC.

There is, however, a degree of flexibility built into the scheme. The commencement of the maternity pay period may be postponed if the woman continues to work past the eleventh week. She cannot claim for any week in which she does any work for her employer and entitlement will start from the week following the one in which she did work.

A woman who works past the eleventh week will receive her full eighteen week entitlement as long as she stops work before the start of the sixth week before the EWC. If she does continue to work beyond the sixth week, she will lose a weeks' SMP for each week or part week she works.

If a woman is confined prior to the eleventh week before the EWC or is confined after the twelfth week but prior to the sixth week before the EWC, and the confinement occurs in a week before that which she has notified as the start of her maternity leave, the first week of her maternity pay period will be one following the week in which she is confined.

Rates of Statutory Maternity Pay

There are two rates of SMP – the *higher* and *lower* rate.

Entitlement to the higher rate will depend on how long the woman has been employed by her employer.

The higher rate is only payable to a woman who has been working continuously for her employer for at least two years into the fifteenth week before the EWC. In addition, she must work, or normally be required to work, sixteen hours per week unless, during a continuous period of five years ending with the qualifying period, her contract of employment normally involved at least eight hours per week.

The higher rate is calculated as 90 per cent of her "normal weekly earnings". The meaning of this phrase is important because it not only fixes the level of the higher rate, but also, as we have seen, determines whether an individual is eligible for SMP in the first place. Where the employee is paid on a weekly basis, the "normal weekly earnings" are the gross average earnings over a period of eight weeks ending with the fifteenth week before the EWC. If the employee is paid monthly, all the gross pay received in the two months up to and including the last normal pay day before the qualifying week will count. This sum is then multiplied by six and divided by 52 in order to produce the "normal weekly earnings" figure.

The higher rate of SMP is available during the first six weeks for which SMP is payable. For the remainder of the maternity pay period, the *lower* rate is applicable.

The lower rate will also be payable to those women who are entitled to SMP but who do not fulfil the higher rate conditions described above. The lower rate is currently £36.25 (from 6 April 1988).

SMP as "earnings"

SMP is treated as earnings, so the employer will make any tax or N.I. deductions from the payments that are due. The payments should be made at the same time and at the same interval as the woman's wages would have been paid. On the other hand, there appears to be nothing in the statutory scheme to prevent the payment of SMP as a lump sum. From the employer's point of view, however, this is unwise as it may then prove difficult to recover any overpayment.

When SMP ends

The employer's liability to pay SMP will terminate when the maximum of eighteen weeks' payments have been made. However, it can end earlier if, after confinement, the employee does any work for any employer other than the one for whom she is working in the fifteenth week before the EWC. Should she do this, she loses her right to SMP for that week and the rest of the maternity pay period. In such a case, she is required to notify her original employer within seven days of the date she commenced work.

Employer's failure to pay

The employer is under an obligation, at the request of the employee, to supply a written statement stating the reasons for his refusal to pay all or part of the alleged SMP entitlement. Failure to give such reasons on request is an offence, punishable by a fine of up to £400. If the employee remains dissatisfied with the explanation, she may refer her complaint to a DSS adjudication officer who will decide whether payment is due. Both employer and employee have the right of appeal to a Social Security Appeal Tribunal and, depending on the issue, further rights of appeal to the Social Security Commissioner or the Secretary of State.

Recovery of SMP by employers

Payments may be recovered in the same way as SSP by deducting the amounts so paid from the National Insurance contributions paid by the employer in respect of employees.

Relationship with contractual entitlement

SMP payments may be set-off against wages payable in that week or any payments under an occupational maternity or sick-pay scheme and vice-versa. So if an employer pays maternity pay under an occupational scheme there is no need to pay SMP on top of that. The employer may recover the proportion of maternity pay which corresponds to SMP. Payments other than wages, occupational maternity or sick pay may not be set-off. So if the employee is entitled to holiday pay, SMP may not be deducted from it.

5.8 Reduction in work/lay-off

General rule

As a general rule there is no obligation on the employer to provide work, so long as the *wages* agreed continue to be paid.[29] The principle here is that as long as the employee makes himself available it is up to the employer to decide the amount of work (if any) he wants to provide during that time. There are, though, some important exceptions to this rule. For wages purposes the main one is that there may be an implied obligation to provide work where the opportunity to earn wages depends on this. Examples are where employees are paid by results or on piece-rates[30], or by commission[31].

There may also be situations in which a person has a right to work to enable him to maintain his ability to

---

[29] Unless the contract *authorises* non-payment, reduced earnings etc., (for example because of a shortage of orders) *failing* to pay wages at the agreed level will be a breach of contract; see Bond v CAV Ltd., Neads v CAV Ltd. (1983) IRLR 360.
[30] *Devonald* v *Rosser & Sons* (1906) 2 K.B. 728, C.A.
[31] *Turner* v *Goldsmith* (1891) 1 Q.B. 544; see further on commission pay, pages 17 to 19 above.

make *future* earnings, notably where he needs to practice his skills, maintain his reputation in his trade etc.

☐ *Example*

B. was employed as a sales director under a service agreement for a five year fixed term. Towards the end of the agreement he was told (after disagreements with the company) that he would not be required to work out the remaining time under the contract. It was held that this broke an implied term that he should be able to work in his capacity as sales director. This point was reinforced by the fact that he was paid bonuses based on net profits: although the company had agreed to pay an amount of bonus calculated on the profits until the fixed term expired, he should have had the opportunity to *contribute* to the company's profits by continuing his sales work. The fact that he was a senior manager, and that his reputation could have been damaged if it had become generally known that he was no longer working were also relevant factors.[32]

Authorised lay-off/suspension

The basic rule that staff cannot be laid off without pay (or otherwise have their earnings reduced) when there is a reduction of work available can, of course, be overcome by implied[33] or express conditions to the contrary. It is not uncommon in many industries to insert clauses in employees' contracts which provide for a temporary suspension without pay (or at reduced pay) when there is a shortage of work. There can be a problem, though, in deciding at what point a lay-off has gone on for beyond what could reasonably be regarded as a "temporary" period.

---

[32] *N. F. Bosworth* v *Angus Jowett & Co. Ltd.* (1977) IRLR 374.
[33] *Browning and others* v *Crumlin Valley Collieries Ltd.* (1926) 1 K.B. 522 (where essential colliery repairs had to be carried out).

☐ *Example*
Mrs. Tiffen worked in the rag trade. She was laid off without pay under a clause in her contract which read "if there is a shortage of work, or the firm is unable to operate because of circumstances beyond its control (the company) has the right to lay you off temporarily and without remuneration". It did not define, though, what "temporarily" meant. It was held that in this event (and in similar cases in the future) this should be a matter determined by the industrial tribunal. In the context of the rag trade, where earnings were low (and it was unlikely that employees had adequate savings to see them through a long period without work) it was considered that four weeks was a reasonable maximum time during which an employer could rely on such a clause. As Mrs. Tiffen had been laid off beyond this period she was entitled to regard the employer as in breach of contract, and could claim a redundancy payment.[34]

Temporary transfers

A problem that often arises is where there is a reduction in the work available in part of a business, and in order to avoid immediate redundancy in that area, the staff concerned are asked to transfer to other areas of work.

This can obviously be a better option than redundancy or lay-off, but there are several pitfalls as far as wages are concerned. Unless it is clearly within management's power to instruct employees to transfer (for example because of mobility provisions in a collective agreement), it is preferable to proceed with such arrangements by agreement. Apart from this being a desirable approach anyway, particularly if people are being transferred to less skilled work, it is generally necessary to make it clear that such transfers are temporary and will not involve a reduction in earnings.

[34] *A. Dakri & Co. Ltd.* v *Tiffen and others* (1981) IRLR 57; on redundancy payments, see EPCA ss.81, 83.

☐ *Example*
Highly skilled sewing machinists who worked in an upholstery department were asked to transfer to less skilled work in another department. This was only intended by the company as a temporary measure and they were told their earnings would be the same. But when they asked for clarification of these points they were given an ultimatum to accept the transfer immediately or leave. They left and successfully claimed unfair dismissal and redundancy payments. Firstly, the employers had not explained how long the transfer was to last – simply stating that it would be until the work in the upholstery department picked up again meant it could be an unlimited (or at least very uncertain) period. Secondly, the promise that wages would be the same was ambiguous given that pay was calculated in a different way in their new department, and was very dependent on bonuses being paid. The promise could have been more of a *forecast* as to their future earnings rather that a guarantee (which is what they were entitled to expect.[35]

Collective agreements

Although there is now a statutory scheme of minimum guarantee payments (see pages 89 to 91 below), there are many industries which have national agreements providing for payments during periods of lay-off and short-time working. Similarly many employers negotiate such arrangements "in-house" with their unions. Where this is the case it is possible for employers to be exempted from the operation of the statutory requirements.[36] Even if no exemption has been given, any payments made by the employer under the contract

[35] *Millbrook Furnishing Industries Ltd.* v *McIntosh & others* (1981) IRLR 309.
[36] EPCA s.18; there must, however, be provision for the referral of disputes over payments to independent arbitration or the industrial tribunal (s.18(4)).

of employment for a workless day will go towards discharging liability to pay statutory payments. [37]

One of the advantages of such collective agreements is that they can be tailored to suit the needs of the particular industry concerned. The benefits provided will generally be better than those laid down by the legislation, and further improvements can be periodically re-negotiated. To some extent they also enable the employer to introduce *restrictions* on the making of payments. An example would be that payments are not payable where employees are laid off as a result of industrial action in another plant in the same industry. The effect of such conditions, though, will be something for the courts and tribunals to determine.

☐ *Example*

An engineering national agreement provided for guaranteed employment and pay. But it also said that the guarantee would be suspended if the reduction in work was due to industrial action in a federated establishment. N. was laid off following a dispute in another department in the same factory. However, he was able to show that work which he normally did was still available for him. He successfully sued for his normal wages. The employer could not rely on the national agreement as that only applied where work was unavailable to the particular employee – it did not create a general right to lay off staff when there was industrial action. Nor was there a custom in the industry allowing employers to lay off workers in these circumstances.[38]

---

[37] EPCA s.16 (2); and see *Cartwright* v *G. Clancy Ltd.* (1983) ICR 552 (employers relieved from paying any statutory payments in a three month period once they had paid five days of payments under their own scheme, see further, page 90 below).

[38] *Bond* v *CAV Ltd., Neads* v *CAV Ltd..* (1983) IRLR 360.

Statutory payment

Even if an employee is not entitled to pay under his contract, he may nevertheless qualify for a *statutory guarantee payment*,[39] although these are not over-generous.

Payments are made where there has been a "workless day". This is where work is not provided on a day on which the employee would normally be working (and does not) as a result of either:

☐ a *diminution in the requirements of the business* for work which the employee is employed to do; or

☐ any *other occurrence affecting the employer's business* in relation to work of the kind the employee is employed to do . . .

For the purpose of the latter an "occurrence" would include such things which are generally outside the employer's control like a shortage of orders, breakdown in supplies, or power cuts.

Qualifying rules

To claim a payment the employee must have been continuously employed for a period of not less than one month ending with the day for which payment is claimed.[40]

If he is employed under a fixed term contract of three months or less; or a contract which is for a task which is not expected to last for more than three months, he must have been continuously employed for a period of more than three months ending with the day payment is claimed for.[41] This clearly excludes many casual workers from a right to payments.

---

[39] EPCA ss.12 to 18.
[40] EPCA s.13 (1).
[41] EPCA s.13 (2).

An employer does *not* have to make a payment in the following situations:[42]

☐ if the failure to provide work is due to a strike, lockout or other industrial action involving another employee of that employer, or an associated employer's employee;

☐ the employee refuses suitable alternative employment (which need not, necessarily, be work he is employed to do under this contract); or

☐ the employee does not comply with reasonable requirements to ensure his services are available.

Calculating the payment

Detailed rules are set out in the legislation[43], but basically the payment is calculated by multiplying the number of normal working hours in the workless day by the *guaranteed hourly rate*. The figure is arrived at by dividing one week's pay (including any contractual additional payments like bonuses, or regular overtime) by the hours that have been worked. If the hours vary each week an average number of hours taken over a twelve week period (ending with the last full week before the day claimed for) is used. In any event a guarantee payment cannot exceed a fixed level (currently £11.30), and this can be paid for up to a maximum of five days in any three month period. If the employee's normal working week is less that five days, the maximum number of days will be the same as that figure. Thus a four day week will mean a maximum of *four* payments in a three month period.

As already noted (page 88 above) any contractual payments made for workless days will off-set any statutory liability to make payments. In practice, though, such payments are usually greater than the statutory

[42] EPCA s.13 (3), (4).
[43] EPCA ss.14 to 16.

minimum so they are essentially a "topping-up" payment over and above the statutory requirements. Payments from sources *other* than the employer (e.g. private insurance, union assistance, etc.) do *not* affect the statutory payment.

Complaints to a tribunal

A complaint may be made to a tribunal that guarantee payments have not been paid. This must be done within three months of the workless day.[44]

5.9 Industrial action

Right to dismiss/stop paying wages

Industrial action can take a variety of forms, ranging from an "all-out" stoppage of work for an uncertain period of time to "non co-operation" by an individual employee. The basic principle – which was referred to in a 1987 House of Lords case[45] – is that any form of action which is intentionally causing harm to the employer's business will entitle the employer to treat the contract as at an end, and enable him to dismiss the employee.

If the employer elects to take this course of action the obligation to pay wages will, of course, end as from the time of dismissal. It would not resume again unless the employee was reinstated. Negotiated "return to work" arrangements do sometimes provide for wages to be paid in arrears from the date of reinstatement and these can provide for full continuity of wages, employer's national insurance and pension contributions, etc., or for partial payment of wages.

The practical problems involved in wages administra-

---

[44] EPCA s.17.
[45] *Miles* v *Wakefield District Council* (1987) 1 All E.R. 1089 at 1097; IRLR 193 at 199.

tion (and, no doubt, industrial relations considerations) in dealing with dismissals and reinstatements will often prompt the employer *not* to exercise the dismissal option. In this case there are a number of other courses of action which may be pursued, and most of these involve withholding all or part of the wages that would otherwise be due but for the industrial action.

Before looking at those options it should be pointed out that while an employee is taking industrial action he will be precluded from bringing a complaint to the industrial tribunal. The rule which establishes this is the EPCA s.62, which will apply even where the employee's action would not normally involve a breach of contract.

☐ *Example*
Mr Faust and two colleagues refused to work overtime when asked. Although they were not contractually obliged to do so (so that they would normally be quite entitled to refuse), their reason was their support for a ban on overtime connected with wage negotiations. It was held that in these circumstances their action constituted "industrial action" and they were therefore prevented from complaining to the industrial tribunal.[46]

Recovering damages

Although there may be cases in which it is not clear whether a "work-to-contract", "go-slow", etc., involves a breach of contract on the part of the employee, most forms of industrial action are regarded by the courts as doing so. If the action *does* amount to a breach of contract the employer is entitled to sue for damages for the loss of services that would otherwise have been provided had the employee been working normally.

☐ *Example*
A collective agreement between the coal pit deputies'

[46] *Power Packing Casemakers Ltd.* v *Faust & Others* (1983) 1 Q.B. 471, C.A.

union (NACODS) and the coal board allowed the management to require deputies to work on "such days or part days in each week as may reasonably be required . . . " As a result of industrial action involving a refusal to work on Saturday shifts, the board had to employ subsititute workers to maintain production. Mr Galley, one of the deputies taking the action, was held to be liable to pay damages for breach of his contract. These were assessed on the basis of the loss of output caused by his failure to work, although on the facts of the case this did not amount to more than the cost of providing a substitute for him.[47]

In practice it is now uncommon for employers to resort to this option.

Suspension

There is no general right to suspend an employee without pay. An employer can only take such action if the contract authorises it. He must also follow any procedural steps that may be laid down in the suspension procedure (such as warnings or consultations).

If an agreement provides for suspension but the employer makes it clear by his action, letters sent to staff, etc., that he is not invoking that right, then it may be harder at a later stage to justify withholding pay. This was the case, for example, when in response to a union instruction teachers refused to accept additional pupils into their classes.[48] Rather than dismiss the teachers concerned (or invoke the suspension procedure provided for), the education authority allowed them to continue working with classes of the existing size. In

---

[47] *National Coal Board* v *Galley* (1958) 1 All E.R. 91; see also *Gaumont-British Picture Corporation Ltd.* v *Alexander* (1936) 2 All E.R. 1686 where it was held that an actress who had refused to perform a part (and who was not paid accordingly) was also liable to pay damages.

[48] *Royle* v *Trafford BC* (1984) IRLR 184; and cf *Cresswell and others* v *Board of Inland Revenue* (1984) IRLR 190.

these circumstances the authority could not (as it had claimed the right to do) rely on the suspension power to make deductions (based on an assessment of the damage caused) which meant that a teacher effectively received no salary at all during the period of action. The court did recognise, though, that a small proportion of the arrears of wages due should be withheld, and this was based on a notional valuation of the services not provided.

Deductions during industrial action

The case referred to in the last section made it clear that the court, when considering an employee's claim for arrears of pay during a period of industrial action, could decide that a proportion of those arrears may be *held back* by the employer. In fact, had more extensive loss been shown by the employer a *larger* proportion (up to, perhaps, *all* the arrears) might have been withheld.

In a later situation in which an education authority withheld wages (when teachers were refusing to provide "cover" when their colleagues were absent) it has been clearly established that an employer *can* do this to the extent that the deductions *do* realistically represent a proper estimate of the loss caused by the action.[49]

The problem in many cases is in deciding what *is* a fair deduction to make. This can be a particular problem where, for example, the action does not involve an actual withdrawal of labour (such as a "work to rule", or a refusal to operate new working practices, or where the employee refuses to perform *part* of his contractual duties, but otherwise continues to substantially carry out his job.[50] In these situations the deduction is liable

---

[49] *Sim* v *Rotheram MBC* (1986) 3 WLR 851; note the Wages Act 1986 requirements (see page 129) do not apply where a deduction is made in respect of a strike or "industrial action" (s.1 (5) of the 1986 Act).

[50] In this latter case it is not possible to stop paying any wages at all, unless the contract authorises this; *Wilusznski* v *Tower Hamlets L.B.C.* (1988) IRLR 154.

to be arbitrary or excessive and would, of course, have to be justified if the employee then sued for arrears. The position is easier where the action involves a withdrawal of labour, as in the case of one-day strikes, or refusal to perform duties for a given period while at work. Here, a deduction based *pro rata* on the employee's normal weekly hours can normally be made. The position here, which was recently confirmed by the House of Lords, is "no work, no pay".[51]

☐ *Example*

Mr Miles, was a Superintendent Registrar of births, deaths and marriages in Wakefield. Although he was an "office-holder" (see page 8 above) who held office at the pleasure of the Registrar General his salary was paid by Wakefield Council. He worked a thirty-seven hour week, which included three hours on a Saturday morning. In support of industrial action by his union he refused to carry out part of his duties on Saturdays, namely conducting weddings. The Council made it clear that it did not accept this as proper performance of his duties and he was not, therefore, paid for his Saturday work. He tried, unsuccessfully, to recover this pay. It was held:

(a) that his position was so similar to that of somebody working under a contract of employment that his case would be decided as if he were an employee;

(b) he had only offered to perform *part* of his duties and, in response, the council was entitled to reject this and not pay for the part that was not being performed; and

(c) employees (and office-holders like Mr. Miles) were only entitled to recover wages if they were able to show they were willing to carry out *their* obligations.

[51] *Miles* v *Wakefield MDC* (1987) 1 All E.R. 1089; (1987) IRLR 193 H.L.

5.10 Change in working methods; new technology

General principles

There will, inevitably, be times when an employer will want changes to be made in the way a job is done. Such change may be dictated by a management identifying more efficient and cost-effective methods of working, or simply as a the result of new technology providing alternative ways of carrying out the work.

As a general rule an employer is entitled to require an employee to adapt to changes if doing so is allowed for in the contract of employment. This would obviously be so where the contract specifically *says* that staff can be moved to different work or be re-trained to carry out new skills, tasks etc. Even without such express terms, though, the law expects a fair degree of flexibility to be shown when changes in working methods are called for.

The introduction of new working methods and technology can often be a cause of friction between employers and staff. As far as wages are concerned such situations create a number of possibilities. If the proposed changes represent no more than a different way of doing what remains as essentially the *same work* then the employee will be obliged to *adapt* to such changes. A refusal to do so will entitle the employer to withhold pay.

☐ *Example*
Staff working for the Inland Revenue were responsible for the administration of the PAYE ("Pay As You Earn") system. Much of that work had been done manually, sending out notifications of changes in PAYE coding, etc. The Inland Revenue then introduced, in several areas, a computerised system which could do much of the arithmetical work of making alterations, and sending out revised codings. It was still possible, however, for a tax officer to handle

individual "problems" in the traditional manual way should this be necessary. Training in the use of the new system was provided – an expense which employers are normally obliged to meet. On union instructions the staff refused to operate the new system, although they said they were still willing to carry on working using manual methods. The Inland Revenue made it clear that they would not accept this, and that staff would not be paid while they refused to operate the new system.

In the High Court proceedings the staff argued that this amounted to "suspension" without pay, and that this could not be done unless certain procedures (which had not been followed) were complied with. In any case, they said, the Board were not contractually entitled to require them to work the new system.

The Court, however, rejected their claim. The main point was that, despite computerisation, their job remained essentially the same. Although it was done in a different *way* the new requirements had not posed any substantial difficulties in terms of the training and instruction required, or in putting the system into practice. As working with the computerised system was within the scope of the duties staff could be expected to perform, the principle "no work, no pay" applied. The Board were therefore entitled to withhold pay until employees showed themselves ready to work with the new equipment. Nor did the Board's actions amount to "suspension" (which would have meant various procedural steps should have been taken), as the Board had always undertaken to pay the staff if they carried out their duties.[52]

Need to re-negotiate wages

There might, of course, be situations in which the proposed change in working methods and practices *is* so

[52] *Cresswell and others* v *Board of Inland Revenue* (1984) IRLR

radically different from what is envisaged in the contract that an employee *would* be entitled to refuse to accept the change. In this case the employer would have to *re-negotiate* the contract in question – either with the individual concerned or, perhaps, in the form of a collective agreement that applied to the staff in question. This might provide for extra payments for using new technology, re-gradings, etc.

Alternatively, an employer might be able to justify dismissal of staff not co-operating with proposed changes. This would require him to show that the changes were for a "substantial reason" (such as an essential business reorganisation) and that he acted reasonably in treating it as a sufficient reason for dismissing the employee.[53] (See, further, the cases referred to in page 117 below.)

Redundancy

In situations in whch the content of an employee's job has been reduced a *redundancy* may occur, entitling him to a redundancy payment.[54] To qualify, though, it must be shown that the requirements for the employee to carry out work of a particular kind where he is employed have "ceased or diminished" (or are expected to so do).[55] Whether or not this has happened can be a difficult question. It would not apply where work was simply *reorganised*. An example of this is a change from night working to day-time shifts (which can, of course, have the effect of reducing overtime earnings of the staff affected). In this instance it has been decided that staff are unable to claim redundancy payments if the need to carry out the work has *not* been reduced.[56] In deciding

---

[53] EPCA ss.57 (1), (3).
[54] EPCA ss.81 (1), (2) (b); see, further, on redundancy, Marsh Ch. 13.
[55] EPCA s.81 (2) (b).
[56] *Lesney Products & Co. Ltd.. v G. Nolan & Others* (1977) IRLR 77.

whether a redundancy situation has arisen a careful examination must be made of the contract of employment to see exactly what kind of work the employee can be required to do – this might show that he can be expected to undertake a much wider range of duties than he in practice already carries out.[57]

5.11 Time off from work

General principles

During his normal working hours an employee must be available at all times to carry out his work. So subject to any *statutory* rights to time off (which are described below), this means that he must either have a *contractual* right, or else permission, to be away from work.

There may be circumstances where it would be reasonable (particularly in larger companies) to imply a right to leave for short periods, for example to deal with domestic emergencies.[58] A right to time off might also be inferred for particular purposes on the basis of past practice in the workplace or in the industry. If the purpose was work-related (like a training course) it should be paid leave.

Statutory rights

As part of the minimum rights provided by employment legislation employees are given rights to time off for certain prescribed purposes. Although this may only be a right to *unpaid* leave in some cases, paid leave is often given in such cases by collective agreements or as workplace practice.

---

[57] *Haden Ltd.* v *Cowen* (1982) IRLR 314.
[58] *Warner* v *Barbers Stores* (1978) IRLR 109 (where it was held that such a right did not exist in relation to a small business). Such rights would normally be to take *unpaid* leave.

Public duties

An employee who is a magistrate, or who is a member of any of the following, namely: a local authority; statutory tribunal; health authority or family practitioner committee; the managing or governing body of a maintained educational establishment; or water authority, is entitled to reasonable time off.[59] What is "reasonable" for this purpose will depend on the particular circumstances, but regard must be had, in particular, to the duties involved, whether time off is already being given for trade union work (see below), and the circumstances of (and effect of absence on) the business. Leave in this case is unpaid.

Trade union officials

An officer (including a lay-officer like a shop steward) of an independent trade union which is recognised for collective bargaining purposes by the employer must be given reasonable time off[60] for:

- ☐ carrying out duties concerned with industrial relations between the employer (or any associated employer) and their employees; or

- ☐ for industrial relations training which is relevant to carrying out those duties, and which is approved by the TUC or his union.

Time off must be paid at the rate he would have received had he been at work. If his pay varies with the amount of work done, an amount is to be calculated by reference to the average hourly earnings for that work: if a fair estimate cannot be made of his earnings, average earnings of somebody in a comparable job with the same employer can be used.[61] Failing that, a figure which is reasonable in the circumstances may be applied.

[59] EPCA s.29.
[60] EPCA s.27.
[61] EPCA ss.27 (3), (4).

The amount of time off to be permitted, and the purposes for which it must be given, is a question of what is "reasonable in all the circumstances",[62] but in deciding this, regard must be paid to the ACAS *Code of Practice* (1977) on the subject. The tribunals' approach to time off for industrial relations purposes has been generous. Thus, industrial relations is not, for this purpose, limited to obvious functions like meetings with management – it can extend to a much wider range of activities including meetings between the official and other members.[63] The code itself lists a variety of matters including meetings with other union officials, representing constituents (including representation before outside tribunals and bodies), and informing constituents about the progress of negotiations. These activities might also necessitate the provision of facilities like a telephone, accommodation for meetings, etc.

As far as courses are concerned, these must not be so wide-ranging that it is irrelevant to the carrying out of the official's particular industrial relations duties – if it is, there is no obligation to pay for any time off that is given.[64] The subject matter of the course need not necessarily be something which is negotiable with management. Thus a training scheme on staff pensions could qualify for paid time off even where there is limited employee involvement in pensions matters at the official's workplace.[65]

---

[62] EPCA s.27 (2).
[63] *Sood* v *GEC Elliott Process Automation Ltd.* (1979) IRLR 416 at 419, 420. C.f., though, *British Bakeries (Northern) Ltd.* v *Adlington and others* (1988) IRLR 177, EAT (employers not required to pay for time off at meeting to discuss repeal of protective legislation in the industry).
[64] *Menzies* v *Smith & McLaurin Ltd.* (1980) IRLR 180.
[65] *Young* v *Carr Fasteners Ltd.* (1979) IRLR 420.

Trade union activities

Unpaid time off must be given to staff, who are members of a union recognised by the employer, to carry out union activities.[66] The purpose behind this provision is to enable union members to participate effectively in their union's work, and to improve the conduct of industrial relations (see ACAS *Code of Practice 3*.) The amount of time to be allowed will depend on what is reasonable in all the circumstances having regard to the Code. These would include, for example, the operational requirements of small firms.

Safety representatives

Work place safety representatives must be given reasonable time off (which must be paid) in accordance with the Safety Representatives and Safety Committees Regulations 1977.[67] This extends to paid time off for necessary training for this purpose.[68]

Redundant employees

An employee who has been made redundant is entitled, before his notice period expires, to reasonable time off (which must be paid) to look for other work and to arrange training courses.[69] He must have been continuously employed for two years to qualify.

---

[66] EPCA s.28.
[67] S.I. 1977 No. 500. The Schedule deals with pay and its calculation, but this is broadly similar to the system for TU officials' pay (see page 100 above).
[68] See HSC Code of Practice "Safety Representatives and Safety Committees" (1978) and *White* v *Pressed Steel Fisher* (1980) IRLR 176 (paid time off for TU courses may be unnecessary if employer makes adequate in-company provision).
[69] EPCA s.31.

Ante-natal care

A pregnant employee who has, on the advice of a registered medical practitioner, midwife or health visitor, made an appointment to receive ante-natal care, has a right not to be unreasonably refused paid time off for this purpose.[70]

Jury service

Employers are obliged to release staff who are summoned to jury service.[71] Jurors receive travelling and subsistence allowances, and are reimbursed for loss of earnings up to a prescribed maximum limit.

Territorial army, reservists, etc.

Employees who are members of the Territorial Army (and its equivalent in the other armed services) do not enjoy any special statutory rights on time off (and pay during time off) when they attend training sessions. This will therefore always be a matter for agreement between the employer and the individual. Reservists who are liable to call-up and training must, however, be given time off, although there is no obligation to provide *paid* leave. The main legislation dealing with such personnel is the Reserve Forces Act 1980 and advice on their employment can be obtained from the Ministry of Defence.

5.12 Miscellaneous wages problems

Overpayments

If an employee is mistakenly overpaid, the question of whether the overpayment can be recovered will depend

[70] EPCA s.31A.
[71] Juries Act 1974.

on a number of factors. If it is a *factual* misunderstanding – for example as to the hours he has worked, his pay-scale, etc. – there will generally be no problem in insisting on repayment, and, failing that, obtaining judgement for the money in a legal action.

If, on the other hand, the overpayment is made as a result of a mistake in understanding and applying the *law* (for example, in dealing with regulations or statutory provisions) the rule is that it is *not* recoverable.[72] This rule was applied, for example, in the case of an overpayment of a retirement gratuity to a Royal Air Force officer when the relevant statutory order was not applied properly.[73]

In some circumstances it may be impossible to recoup payments even where these are a result of a factual mistake. Thus, in a case where a teacher received £1007 worth of sick payments more than he should have done (because of an error in feeding incorrect information to the computerised payroll), legal action to force repayment failed.[74] The court decided that in cases where an employee could show that:

☐ he had been led to believe the money was his;

☐ he had, in good faith and without knowing about the employer's claim, been affected by the payment (for example by incurring expenditure or losing social security benefits); and

☐ the overpayment was not primarily his fault,

the claim to repayment will fail. On overpayment of commission, and expenses of people paid on commission, see Ch.2.2 above and footnote 34 thereto.

---

[72] *R. E. Jones Ltd.* v *Waring and Gillow Ltd.* (1926) A.C. 670, 688, 698.
[73] *Holt* v *Markham* (1923) 1 K.B. 504.
[74] *Avon County Council* v *Howlett* (1983) 1 All E.R. 1073, C.A.

Employee's criminal liability

In exceptional cases, where it is clear that the employee has deliberately held on to an overpayment *knowing* that he is not entitled to keep it, a prosecution under the Theft Act 1968[75] is possible. This was established following a case in which a police officer was mistakenly overpaid (by direct debit into her bank account) for wages and overtime to which she was not entitled.[76]

Making deductions

The restrictions on making deductions from employees pay that are in the Wages Act 1986 do not apply when these are made to reimburse the employer for overpayments (see page 132 below).

Reimbursing employees' expenditure

If an employee incurs expenditure in order to carry out his work the general rule is that he is entitled to be reimbursed for this.[77] This is only a term which is implied when it is clear that no other specific arrangements have been agreed – these might, for example, make the *employee* responsible for overheads, costs, etc.

The right to be reimbursed for costs will, in any case, only extend to expenditure which is reasonably incurred. It obviously does not cover situations where the employee is acting outside the scope of his employment, has gone beyond his instructions, etc. A press officer who libelled people in a press statement could not, for example, claim his legal costs if sued.[78]

---

[75] S.1 in combination with s.5 (4).
[76] *Attorney-General's Reference (No. 1 of 1983)* (1984) 3 All E.R. 369.
[77] *In re Famatina Development Corporation Ltd.* (1914) 2 Ch. 271.
[78] *Clitherow's Trustee* v *Hemingway* (1966) 116 NLJ 1004; (1966) CLY 4433.

Working for other employers

Contracts of service (or for services) can restrict staff's ability to work and receive earnings from other employers. In any case obligations which are implied in all contracts – including the duty of "fidelity" – can operate to prevent them benefiting from work undertaken in the employer's time, or which competes with his business. In some circumstances staff can be required to account to their employer for their earnings. Employers will also be entitled to earnings from inventions, designs, etc, subject to any specific contractual provisions in each case, and rights under the Patents Act 1977.

5.13 State assistance with wages

The three most important forms of State assistance for those on low wages are Family Credit, Income Support, and Housing Benefit. Further help with expenditure which cannot be met out of earnings can be obtained from grants or loans from the Social Fund (see, further, *Cash Help While You're Working* (DHSS FB4)).

☐ *Family Credit*
This is available to employees and self employed staff, and it is payable to families (including single-parent ones) where there is a child under 16 (or 19 if still in full-time education). The earner must be working more than 24 hours a week, and the benefit is not dependant on national insurance contributions. The present earnings level, below which earners qualify, is £96.50 net earnings per week. The precise entitlement will depend on the family's income. Savings or capital of over £6000 will mean disqualification; and amounts over £3000 will reduce the amount of entitlement. See, further, *Family Credit* (Leaflet FC1).

☐ *Income Support*
This is payable to earners who are over 16. It is only paid if applicants (or their partner) work less than 24 hours a week. The same savings rule applies as with Family Credits (see above). The benefit is not dependent on N.I. Contributions, but it is means-tested so that income from other sources will be taken into account. Payments consist of a personal allowance; allowances for children; premium amounts (for any special expenses); and housing costs not met by housing benefit, e.g. mortgage interest payments. See, further, *A Guide to Income Support* (SB22).

☐ *Housing Benefit*.
This is an income benefit paid by local authorities to people on low wages who require help with rent and rates. It is not paid to homeowners with mortgage responsibilities. Those receiving Income Support will normally also qualify for Housing Benefit. To determine exact entitlement, reference is made to earnings, unearned income, and any savings between £3000 and £6000. See, further, Leaflet RR1 – *Housing Benefit*.

Chapter 6

CHANGES IN WAGES

Part I – Changes by the parties

6.1 Introductory points

In most cases wages – and the way in which they are to be calculated, paid, etc. – are fixed when the employment begins. At that stage employers and employees rarely make any kind of formal agreement or arrangements on how future changes might take place. The problem this creates, of course, is that unless there *is* some such procedure then changes *cannot* normally be made without both parties *agreeing* on this. Something which may be difficult or impossible to achieve, at least without some blood-letting on both sides!

Agreeing changes with unions/staff

If agreement is reached with a union which represents the staff affected by a change, new system, etc., then agreed changes will normally be binding on each of those staff (see pages 36, 54, 55 above) without the need for reaching any further agreement with every individual concerned. This would *not* be the case, however, where the individuals have *withdrawn* the union's authority to negotiate changes on their behalf.

☐ *Example*
After S. resigned from the union an agreement between management and union was reached introducing new shift arrangements. S. refused to accept this and was able to successfully claim that his existing contractual terms continued unchanged. The

agreement did not affect S.'s contract as the union no longer negotiated on his behalf.[1]

In the case of non-union staff, they will be bound by any arrangements negotiated between their employer and the union if there is a clause in their contract which states that their terms and conditions will be in accordance with such agreements; or possibly, if there is an implied term or customary understanding that they are bound. Otherwise, agreement *will* have to be reached with each of them individually if a change that affects their contractual rights is to be introduced.

Pay increases and reductions

In practice increases in wages (or other reorganisation in the method of paying them which benefits the employee) are the result of either the employer deciding to award them unilaterally, or else occur after negotiations ending in agreement. Although annual pay negotiations and annual pay have become a normal practice in most industries, there is no legal requirement either to negotiate or pay an annual rise (although see page 57 above). There are no other legal requirements dealing with the re-negotiation of wages (for example, requiring an employer to regularly review or discuss wages, negotiate in good faith, etc.). If the employer recognises a trade union for collective bargaining purposes, he must provide it with any relevant information they need, for example, on the company's performance and profits. [2] *Reductions* in wages can only, as a rule, be made after agreement between employer and employee (or a union acting on his behalf).

Having made these general points it is necessary to consider in a bit more detail the following aspects of the problem. Namely:

[1] *C. Singh* v *British Steel Corporation* (1974) IRLR 131.
[2] Employment Protection Act 1975 ss.17 to 21; and see ACAS *Code of Practice No. 2* on Disclosure of Information to Trade Unions (1977) for detailed guidance.

(6.2) the possibility that the contract *permits* variations to be made without the employee's consent;

(6.3) situations in which employees might be *treated* as accepting changes, even though they have not expressly agreed to them;

(6.4) the *responses* an employee can make to attempt to impose variations; and

(6.5) how an employer might '*justify*' imposed changes.

6.2 Permitted variations

It may be the case that the individual's contract of employment expressly authorises changes to be made, for example by specifying some event which can "trigger" a reduction – a down-turn in sales might, therefore, be specified as a reason for reducing a salesman's commission. Similarly, there may be terms providing for changes to take place but only after consultations with unions, or after the matter has been through other procedures in a firm's collective bargaining machinery. Whether the power to make changes requires agreement or not may depend on the wording of the particular contract or agreement (as in the *Miller* case, page 112 below).

Although, in theory it might be possible to *imply* a right to alter wages (or rely on an orally-agreed term to do so), in practice this is unlikely to be supported by the courts. Custom and practice, as a basis of authority for making reductions, is not generally recognised – see the cases referred to on pages 60 to 61 above. The withdrawal of pay entitlements might, in exceptional circumstances, be authorised by Statute (see p. 65 above).

Minor changes; method of computation

Although there is some authority for the view that minor reductions in pay might not be sufficiently significant to justify an employee leaving (and then, complaining of constructive dismissal),[3] the better view is that *any* reduction will normally amount to a repudiation of the contract.

Alterations by the employer in the *method* of computation of earnings, even if this does not involve an immediate or significant change in the level of earnings, will similarly be treated as unacceptable. In *R. F. Hill Ltd.* v *Mooney*[4] a salesman's contract gave him the right to a salary plus 1 per cent commission on sales. Later, the company substituted a commission payable on sales over a given target figure. His claim for constructive dismissal was upheld by the EAT. The fact that this introduced a formula, whose exact operation was uncertain at the time it was introduced, was an important factor.

"Severable" elements

There may be situations in which contract terms dealing with pay are "divisible", with some parts (particularly those dealing with supplementary pay benefits) being terminable on reasonable notice being given by the employer.[5] But this may be difficult for the employer to establish. The contention that this could be done in order to terminate a six day guarantee payment scheme for dock workers was rejected in *Gibbons* v *Associated British Ports*,[6] as this was regarded as an integral part of the dockers' terms.

Whether agreement is required

In some industries there may be agreements dealing with downturns in production, short-time working, etc. But they can be complex and it is not always clear how

---

[3] *Gillies* v *Richard Daniels & Co. Ltd.* (1979) IRLR 457.
[4] (1981) IRLR 258.
[5] *Land and Wilson* v *West Yorkshire Metropolitan County Council* (1981) IRLR 87.
[6] (1985) IRLR 376 at 380.

far the introduction of temporary changes in such cases requires prior union or employee agreement, or whether they can be imposed simply by giving notice.

In *Miller* v *Hamworthy Engineering Ltd.*[7] an agreement between the company and the union ASTMS provided for "work sharing" as an alternative to redundancy in the event of a reduction in business. The agreement provided for a temporary waiver of rights to pay. Mr Miller initially agreed to a reduction in hours (and pay) and some of this shortfall was made up by government grants. Later, the company wanted to introduce such short-time working again. This time, however, the agreement of the union was not forthcoming notably because of the absence of a government subsidy. The company nevertheless went ahead and introduced a three day week.

Mr Miller successfully claimed for the net loss of wages due during the periods when short-time working had not been agreed to by the union. The Court of Appeal interpreted the collective agreement as requiring prior agreement, either by the individual or his union. Nor did it matter that the majority of other unions in the company supported the move – there was no provision for "majority" decision.

In another case,[8] though, it was held that the employer's right to vary, alter or cancel provisions in the authority's rules was unlimited. The authority *could* therefore, unilaterally withdraw a non-contributory life assurance scheme. The rules did not require *agreement* between the employer and unions, even though consultations might be provided for.

6.3 Acceptance without express agreement

Although there might be cases where it could be said that employees have, acquiesced, in changes to their

---

[7] (1986) IRLR 461.
[8] *Cadoux* v *Central Regional Council* (1986) IRLR 131.

wages[9] the courts have generally been cautious about implying such agreement particularly where the changes are clearly disadvantageous to them.

A protest against attempts to dictate wage reductions will, of course, rebut any assumption of acquiescence, even if the employee remains in his post rather than leaving.[10] The point was also illustrated in one of the famous "dinner lady" cases.

☐ *Example*
An attempt was made to alter the terms and conditions of school dinner ladies (notably by reducing their hours and pay). The argument that they had, by staying in their jobs and accepting lower pay, waived their right to treat their contracts at an end (and thereby implicitly accepted fresh contracts on the reduced terms) was rejected. They had made it clear that they did not accept any changes, and so they were entitled to a declaration that the employer could not unilaterally alter their contracts, and to obtain their arrears of wages.[11]

In most cases it is likely that employees will not want to immediately exercise their right (in the face of a threatened reduction in pay) of treating the contract as at an end, leaving, and then claiming constructive dismissal or breach of contract. Their right, in this situation, of remaining in a post and drawing arrears of wages due is considered below (see page 116), but in the leading case of *Rigby* v *Ferodo Ltd.*[12] (discussed in page 116 below) it was made clear that simply by continuing to work after his wages had been reduced (and accepting lower wages) Mr. Rigby had neither accepted the employer's repudiation of his contract *nor* accepted the reduced terms they sought to impose.

[9] See the discussion in *Jones* v *Associated Tunnelling Co. Ltd.* (1981) IRLR 477.
[10] *Marriott* v *Oxford & District Co-operative Society Ltd.* (No. 2) (1970) 1 Q.B. 186.
[11] *Burdett-Coutts and others* v *Hertfordshire C.C.* (1984) IRLR 91.
[12] (1987) IRLR 516 at 518 to 519, H.L.

Statements of terms

Just as the employee's signature to a statement of terms[13] might, in some circumstances constitute assent to the terms which are set out in the statement, and be something more than merely *evidence* of the terms and conditions on which he is working (see page 53 above) it might be argued that signing an *amending* statement[14] is effective in making contractual changes. This might be particularly so where, for example, reduced wages were later paid over a protracted period without objections by the employee.

It should be remembered, however, that the main purpose of such statements is to confirm the existence, and any later variations to, terms which have *already* been agreed. They should not be regarded as the *means* by which agreement is obtained.[15]

The law permits variations in pay to be notified in a variety of ways, such as by notice-boards or company magazines; or, for example by revising (and then making available for inspection) a collective agreement. If the individual contract states that it incorporates a collective agreement and any later changes to it, this will be an effective change. The fact that a properly-made variation has *not* been notified in accordance with the legislation will not mean that the variation is ineffective.

6.4 Responses to imposed variations

"Constructive dismissal"

In the face of a unilaterally imposed pay reduction (and also possibly, where there is a change in the method of *calculating* pay (see page 111 above), the employee will

---

[13] Statements are required by EPCA Part I; see page 52 above.
[14] EPCA s.4.
[15] See, for example, *Turriff Construction Ltd.* v *Bryant* (1967) II KIR 659.

generally be entitled to terminate the contract on account of the employer's conduct,[16] (and bring a complaint of unfair dismissal before the industrial tribunal). The test in deciding whether the employer's behaviour permits this is whether the conduct is a significant breach going to the root of the contract, or which shows that the employer no longer intends to be bound by one or more essential terms of that contract. At that stage the employee is entitled to treat himself as discharged from any further performance which *he* might owe.[17]

In most cases involving alterations in pay it will be difficult for an employer to go on to justify his action[18] once the employee has satisfied the first stage of an unfair dismissal claim referred to. The possibility that he might be able to do so is considered further below (page 117).

Wrongful dismissal

In some instances it may be possible for an employee (or other person, such as a consultant, working under a contract) to sue for damages for the employer's premature termination of the contract. This will be particularly appropriate in the case of fixed-term contracts – the loss being measured in terms of the deprivation of salary, benefits, etc., that would have been received under the contract in the period remaining to run. More usually, though, damages are based on any notice period stipulated (or reasonably implied) for termination of the contract.

---

[16] EPCA s.55 (2) (c).
[17] See *Western Excavating (ECC) Ltd.* v *Sharp* (1978) ICR 221; (1978) IRLR 27; applied in *R. F. Hill Ltd.* v *Mooney* (1981) IRLR 258 (page 111 above). On constructive dismissal generally, see Marsh Ch. 21.
[18] EPCA s.57 (1) to (3).

Remaining in the job

The employee may, instead of leaving, elect to remain in his job and, after making it clear that he does not accept any changes, take action in the courts. Thus in the *Burdetts-Coutts* case (page 113 above) the dinner ladies were able to recover arrears of wages due. In many respects this must now be regarded as more advisable, from the employee's point of view, than the alternative of leaving and claiming unfair dismissal.

In the more recent House of Lords case of *Rigby* v *Ferodo Ltd.*[19] the employer, having failed to gain union agreement to a wage reduction, simply announced new, reduced, pay rates. Mr Rigby's pay was reduced by some £30 per week. He continued working at the reduced rate but both he (and the union) made it clear that the change had not been agreed to. His claim for damages for breach of contract succeeded at all stages.

In the House of Lords a number of important points were made:

☐ the employer's action, though "repudiatory", did not *automatically* bring the contract to an end – to do that required the employee's *acceptance* that this was the case. Mr Rigby had, in fact, confirmed that he wanted to *stay* in his job;

☐ the damages due were not, therefore, limited to what he was owed during his contractual period of notice, but could cover *all* his continuing losses; and

☐ simply giving him notice of the changes did not amount in itself, to terminating the contract. Even if such a principle in law existed (which was doubtful) on the facts of the case it was clear that the employer wanted to *retain* the workforce.

---

[19] (1987) IRLR 516, H.L.

6.5 Justifying imposed changes

There have been a number of cases where unfair dismissal claims have failed after pay changes have been imposed (or sought) – the employer being able to justify action taken, for example because of a necessary business reorganisation. A key provision in this respect is EPCA section 57(1)(b) which enables the employer to demonstrate "some other substantial reason" in establishing the fairness of his action. It will still be necessary, as a *further* step, to show he *acted reasonably* in treating that reason (or any of the other reasons in section 57 like capability, conduct, redundancy, etc.) as a sufficent one.

The point that an employer may be in breach of contract but nevertheless be able to justify this in unfair dismissal proceedings, is illustrated by several cases.

☐ *Example*
G.'s basic pay was consolidated with a supplement he had been receiving. Thereafter, overtime pay was calculated on the consolidated figure rather than, as previously, his basic rate. However, this breached government pay policy, After consultations, the employers proposed new arrangements involving a reduction. His claim to the tribunal failed. Although he could show constructive dismissal on account of the reduction the dismissal was not "unfair", particularly given the difficulties the company found itself in with the government's pay policy.[20]

In another situation the National Farmer's Union, had offered new terms and conditions to its group secretaries in Cornwall. This was done in order to bring salaries in that area into line with those in the rest of the country.

☐ *Example*
H. objected to the new terms and when he refused to

[20] *Industrial Rubber Products* v *C. Gillon* (1977) IRLR 389.

sign a new contract was dismissed. The tribunal accepted that the dismissal was justified, namely because of a "substantial reason" justified for business reasons. Although the EAT on appeal considered the lack of consultation involved suggested the employers has not acted reasonably, the Court of Appeal adopted a different approach. The employers had established a substantial reason which justified dismissal. The point as to whether dismissal was *justified* did not depend on whether there had been adequate consultation beforehand. Indeed consultation (which in this case was not required before reorganisations took place) was just one of a number of factors to be taken into account by the tribunal, and on all the facts they were entitled to regard the dismissal as fair.[21]

In *Kent County Council* v *Gilham*[22], another case involving changes to dinner ladies' contracts, the Court of Appeal made it clear that whether or not an employer had behaved reasonably in dismissing an employee is a question of fact for tribunals in each case. In this particular case the employers were able to put forward a "substantial reason", namely the need to achieve economies forced on them by a national policy to reduce spending in the public sector: and by offering new contracts on reduced terms to avoid a closure of all (or a major part) of the school's meal service in the area.

Once an employer establishes a reason which *could* justify dismissal this, it was said, passes as a "substantial reason". Thereafter the enquiry moves on to the question of reasonableness for the purposes of section 57(3). On this aspect of the case in hand, though, the tribunal was entitled to decide that the employers had not acted reasonably.

[21] *Hollister* v *National Farmers' Union* (1979) ICR 542. Since the House of Lords decision in *Polkey* v *A.E. Dayton Services Ltd.* (1987) IRLR 503, the importance of proper consultation before dismissal action is considered must be emphasised.
[22] (1985) IRLR 18.

Part II – Changes by virtue of legislation

Reference must now be made to the two most important legislative sources of change to wages, namely wages council orders and equal pay and race discrimination claims.

6.6 Wages Council Orders

Background

The power of wages councils to make orders fixing minimum wages and other conditions in certain industries goes back to the Employment Protection Act 1975. Prior to that, trade boards (and, after 1945, wages councils) could recommend the government to set minimum pay conditions.

The legislation which now governs wages councils and their powers is the Wages Act 1986, Part II, replacing the Wages Councils Act 1979.

Present powers

The 1986 Act maintains any wages councils that were in existence when the old Act was repealed, but there are no powers to establish new wages councils. Nor, any longer, can orders be made in respect of workers under 21. Procedures for abolishing or varying the scope of councils are streamlined,[23] and the Secretary of State has wide powers, for example, to take specific employers (or employers within particular organisations) out of the scope of a wages council's powers.

Wages council orders may fix:[24]

[23] WA s.13
[24] WA s.14

- ☐ a single minimum hourly rate of pay for all time work in any week;
- ☐ a single minimum hourly rate for basic weekly hours, and an overtime rate; and
- ☐ limits on what may be deducted for living accommodation provided by the employer.

They will apply to all the time and piece-workers in the industry which the council covers, whether they are full-time or part-time. Amending orders can be made varying rates and limits in earlier orders.

A specific matter which the wages council must address itself to is the *effect* that any proposed order fixing minimum prescribed rates will have on employment levels, particularly in areas where earnings are below the national average for the kind of work concerned.[25] Other procedural formalities require proposed rates or limits to be published and enable people affected (in particular the employers and workers in the industry) to make representations (normally during a period lasting at least twenty-eight days after publication).[26]

Piece-work

Special arrangements are made[27] for piece-workers, that is to say workers whose pay is calculated by what they produce. The minimum pay set for such workers can, in general, operate to ensure that what they receive is no worse than what could be obtained working a similar period at time rates. The level of pay that can be fixed is determined by reference to the standard of a worker of ordinary competence who has no disability affecting his speed of output. The protection given to piece-workers also extends to maintaining their earnings while they

[25] WA s.14 (6)
[26] WA Schedule 3.
[27] WA s.15

are available for work but no work is actually provided.[28]

Employee's rights; employer's liabilities

If an employee who is covered by a wages council order is paid *less* than the order provides for, he is entitled under his contract to be paid the difference.[29] In practical terms this means that he would, if this were necessary, be able to sue in civil proceedings for any arrears of pay due and for a declaration as to what his pay should be.

An employer may also be *prosecuted* for paying less than the prescribed minimum rates, and, in cases where the evidence supports this, the magistrates' court can order up to two years of arrears to be paid (including, possibly, to other workers in the same firm who may also have been underpaid).[30] Although prosecutions can be brought by the Wages Inspectorate, private prosecutions by the employee are also possible.[31]

6.7 Pay discrimination on race grounds.

It was shown in Chapter 3 that the Race Relations Act 1976 deals with discrimination on racial grounds in relation to the terms on which employment is offered. But the RRA also covers discrimination *once the employment has commenced*. Most significantly it deals with discrimination in wage levels on the grounds of race.[32] Thus if an employer provides a wage increase for all staff

---

[28] WA ss.15 (4), (5).
[29] WA s.16 (1).
[30] WA ss.16 (2) to (6).
[31] For a useful guide, see Turner and Kibling *Private Prosecutions Under The Wages Act 1986 Part II* Legal Action, October 1987, p. 12, and, in general, *Private Prosecutions* Shaw & Sons, 1988.
[32] RRA s.4 (2) (a)

except those in a department where there happens to be by far the highest proportion of black employees, this is likely to be treated as indirect discrimination, subject to the defence of justification (see Chapter 3 on defences, procedure and remedies).

6.8 Equal pay for women

The statutory framework

Note has already been made of the Equal Pay Act 1970 (EPA) in Chapter 3. This is the principal statute dealing with the unequal treatment of women concerning the terms and conditions of their employment (not just their pay). However, this area of the law is also closely tied in with European Economic Community (EEC) law. Firstly, the concept of equal pay for equal work is enshrined by Article 119 of the Treaty of Rome – the "constitution" of the EEC.[33] In addition there are two significant EEC directives: the Equal Pay Directive of 1975 and the Equal Treatment Directive of 1976[34] which are directly enforceable against state or quasi-state bodies like local health authorities and which have required member governments to enact legislation in this field. Also of importance is the *interpretation* of these provisions by the European Court of Justice (ECJ), whose decisions are binding on the English courts.

It should be noted that the Sex Discrimination Act 1975 does make provision for other forms of discrimination during employment which may have an indirect effect on wage levels. Thus, it is unlawful to discriminate against women or married persons in the access given to opportunities for promotion, transfer and training.[35] (A similar provision is found in the RRA.)

---

[33] See *Pickstone and others* v *Freemans PLC* (1987) IRLR 218, C.A.; (1988) 2 All E.R. 803; IRLR 357, H.L.
[34] Dirs 75/117 and 76/207 respectively.
[35] SDA s.6 (2).

Variation of the contract under the EPA[36]

The EPA can only operate when a woman is employed on:

☐ "like work";

☐ "equivalent work"; or

☐ "work of equal value";

to that of a male comparator. Where that is the case and one of the terms of her employment is less favourable than that of the comparator or that comparator has the benefit of a term which is not included in the woman's contract then the Act implies an "equality clause" to *vary* the woman's contract to bring it into line with the man's contract. It achieves this by either varying the term which is less favourable or by incorporating the missing term.[37] It has been established in a well-publicised case involving a canteen cook at a shipyard[38] that an equality clause can operate even where the benefits of the woman's contract, taken *as a whole*, may be as favourable, or *more* favourable than that of the comparator. In this case the canteen cook's basic hourly rate and overtime rates were inferior to those of her male comparators (a painter, a joiner, and a thermal insulation engineer), and despite the fact that she had better provision than them for meal breaks and sickness benefit, the House of Lords ruled that her claim for equal rates of pay and overtime pay must succeed.

Examples of the two forms of variation

☐ *Example 1*
   A man receives £200 per week for doing the same job as a woman who only receives £180 per week. The

---

[36] Note: the EPA can also operate in favour of a man.
[37] EPA s.1 (2).
[38] *Hayward* v *Cammell Laird Shipbuilders Ltd.* (1988) 2 All E.R. 257, H.L.

woman's salary will be "varied" to bring it up to £200 per week.

☐ *Example 2*
A man and a woman doing the same job are both paid a basic wage of £180 per week but, in addition, the man receives a £20 allowance for cleaning up time dating back to when the workforce was a male preserve. The woman's contract will have a clause *added* to pay her the £20 allowance.

The male comparator

Where no male comparator exists there will be no basis for a claim for equal pay. The comparator must be working in the same employment, although this can include another establishment of the employer, or an associated employer where common terms and conditions exist for, at least, the relevant group of employees. An associated employer is one which either controls or is controlled by the woman's employer or is controlled by the same third party as the woman's employer.[39] Furthermore, a woman is entitled to compare herself with a male *predecesssor* in the same post.[40]

Like work

For there to be "like work" the woman and comparator have to be doing work of the *"same* or *broadly similar* nature", with any differences being of no practical importance given the nature and frequency of those differences.[41] Tribunals take a "broad-brush" approach to whether jobs are of a similar nature. In looking at any differences, in the second part of the test, tribunals may

---

[39] s.1 (6).
[40] *Macarthy's Ltd.* v *Smith* (1979) IRLR 316; (1980) IRLR 209 (following ECJ ruling).
[41] s.1 (4).

take into account any special circumstances surrounding apparently similar work. For example, if the comparator handles more valuable materials it places more responsibility on him;[42] as might the fact that a comparator works a night shift on his own as a canteen assistant compared with the woman applicant's day shift.[43] Every case will turn on its facts and what in practice occurs, and not just what is stated in the employment contract.

Equivalent work

There can only be a finding of equivalent work where there has been a Job Evaluation Study (JES) previously undertaken which in terms of the demand made on a worker (under various headings like effort, skill, decision-making), gives the work of a woman equal value to that of a comparator.[44] A JES has traditionally been used to place a workforce's jobs in a ranked order to effect a structured pay system. Many of the methods used (see ACAS *Guide No. 1*) do not directly compare factors such as skill, as stipulated by the Act so it would be open to an employee to challenge a JES on these grounds if he thought it was not sufficiently objective. (For the affects of a JES on *equal value* claims see below.)

Work of equal value

This concept was added to the EPA in 1983 in order to comply with EEC Directive 75/117. It is of fundamental importance, enabling an equal pay claim to succeed even where the work of the woman is of an entirely different nature to that of the comparator. This is so even if another man has identical terms and conditions to her own, (although that man's contract will have to be

[42] *Eaton Ltd.* v *J. Nuttall* (1977) IRLR 71 EAT.
[43] *Thomas and others* v *National Coal Board* (1987) IRLR 451 EAT.
[44] s.1 (5).
[45] *Pickstone* v *Freemans PLC* (1987) IRLR 218; (1988) 2 All E.R. 803, IRLR 357, H.L.

varied if the woman's claim is successful).[45] In an equal value claim a tribunal will order an expert report unless it is satisfied that there are no reasonable grounds for determining that the work is of equal value.[46] The report will assess the two jobs in terms of the demands made, under a number of relevant factors such as effort, skill and decision.[47]

JESs and equal value claims

If a prior JES has accorded a woman's work less value than her chosen comparator, then, in the absence of evidence of sex discrimination in the compiling of the study, the claim will fail. However it has been established that in order to comply with section 1(5) – and be free from the taint of sex discrimination – the JES should be scientifically compiled using the "job factors" method (effort, skill, decision etc.)[48]

Defence of "Genuine Material Factor"

This defence is available to an employer if he can show, on the balance of the evidence, that the difference between the woman and comparator's terms and conditions is genuinely due to a material factor other than sex. For like and equivalent work cases there must also be a "material difference" between the woman and comparator's case, though that is not necessary in an equal value claim.[49] However following an important decision on the meaning of "material difference" in a "like work" case, it is unlikely that "equal value" claims will now be treated any differently in relation to this defence.

In the case of *Rainey* v *Greater Glasgow Health Board*[50]

---

[46] s.2A (1).
[47] s.1 (2) (c).
[48] *Bromley and others* v. *H. and J. Quick* (1988) IRLR 249.
[49] s.1 (3).
[50] (1987) IRLR 26, H.L.

the House of Lords decided that a material difference between the woman and comparator need not just relate to personal factors such as qualifications and experience but could extend to economic factors and business efficiency. It had been decided that the National Health Service would only use "in house" prosthetists and so it was necessary to recruit from the private sector. It was felt that this could only be done by guaranteeing these recruits their salary levels which were higher than the NHS rates received by Mrs. Rainey. The Court held that there was a genuine material difference between Mrs. Rainey and the recruits from the private sector.

Procedure

For a *claimant*, it is now established that there is no time limit for commencing an action.[51] In cases referred to an industrial tribunal by an *employer*, or in certain circumstances the *Secretary of State*, there is a time limit of six months from the time the woman left the employment.[52] It is also possible for a court to refer an equal pay question to a tribunal and no time limit applies. The advantage to a claimant of the lack of a time limit is reduced by the fact that, in addition to variation of the contract, the tribunal can only award arrears of remuneration covering the period of two years before the proceedings were instituted.

If the claimant (or employer) wish, they can request the tribunal or court to refer points of EEC law which are unclear (or on which they feel the United Kingdom legislation is not in line with EEC requirements) to the ECJ for its decision.

---

[51] *British Railways Board* v *Paul* (1988) IRLR 20.
[52] s.2 (4).

Chapter 7

DEDUCTIONS

Reference has already been made in Chapter 5 to situations in which an employer may be entitled to pay less than the agreed wages (see pages 71 to 95 in particular, which deal with reductions in earnings during sickness, lay-off, and industrial action). The legal requirement to *notify* employees of deductions in their itemised pay statement has also been discussed (page 66).

The employer's right, if any, to make *deductions* will depend, principally, on whether these are authorised by the contract, or are agreed to by the employee in advance. This is something now established in the Wages Act 1986. The exact scope of that Act, and the special position of workers in retail employment, must be considered further, however, as must the more important deductions specifically authorised by statute.

7.1 Background: the Wages Act 1986

Until their repeal by the 1986 Act[1] as from 1 January, 1987 the Truck Acts 1831 to 1940 and related Acts provided a statutory framework governing the way in which certain categories of workers were paid, and in restricting the making of deductions. In particular they outlawed deductions that amount to "fines".[2] As well as excluding many groups of employees from their scope (for example if they were not "workmen" or, for the purposes of some restrictions "shop assistants"[3]), the

[1] WA ss.11, 32 (2), 33 (5), Schs. 1,5 (Part III); SI 1986 No. 1998.
[2] TA 1896. s.1; *Sealand Petroleum Co. Ltd.* v *Barratt* (1986) 2 All E.R. 360.
[3] TA 1896, s.1 (3); *Bristow* v *City Petroleum Ltd.* (1985) 3 All E.R. 463; (1987) 2 All E.R. 45 H.L.

protection they afforded was very piecemeal.

Despite the shortcomings of the Truck Acts, it might have been expected that they would be replaced by a better system of statutory regulation rather than just repealing them outright. It was decided, however, that the interests of employers and workers would be best served by *deregulation*, and by generally leaving the manner of payment, deductions, etc., to be determined in the contract.[4] Whether this *laissez-faire* approach to deductions can adequately protect groups of workers who are particularly vulnerable to exploitation by unfair contractual conditions remains to be seen.

7.2 Deductions and payments

Basic rules

The present position[5] is that an employer may not make any deduction from any wages of a worker he employs unless the deduction is either:

☐ required or authorised to be made by a *statutory provision* (see pages 144 to 147 for discussion of the main examples), or by any *relevant provision of the worker's contract* (see further, page 132 below); or

☐ the worker has *previously signified in writing* his agreement or consent to the making of it.[6]

Nor may he receive any payment from a worker he employs unless one of these conditions is met.[7] There

---

[4] For the policy of the 1986 Act, see H.L. Debates, Vol. 477, Col. 189 (24.6.86); see (1986) *Public Law* 551 (Sandra Fredman).
[5] WA s.1 (1); for official guidance on the Act, see *The Law on the Payment of Wages and Deductions* (Dept. of Employment PL 810).
[6] Even if the deduction is authorised in this way, the employee must be *notified* of it in the itemised pay statement (see page 66 on this). On compensation limits, though, see page 138.
[7] WA s.1 (2).

may be an exception to this where it could be said that the payment was not received by the employer in his capacity as an employer but in some other capacity, such as an agent for another party, on a social occasion, etc.[8]

"Wages"

For the purposes of these requirements wages are widely defined to mean "any sums payable to the worker by his employer in connection with his employment".[9] Specifically within the definition are:

> "any fee, bonus, commission, holiday pay or other emolument referable to his employment, whether payable under his contract or otherwise".

and payments like Statutory Sick Pay, Statutory Maternity Pay, and guarantee payments. Also included are payments in the nature of a non-contractual bonus[10] and benefits in kind like vouchers or stamps which have a fixed value expressed in monetary terms and can be exchanged for money, goods or services.[11] Examples would be luncheon vouchers and gift tokens. Excluded from the definition[12] and therefore excluded from the requirements of section 1 are:

- ☐ payments by way of an *advance under a loan agreement* or by way of an *advance of wages* – but this will not prevent the restrictions in section 1 applying to deductions made from wages in respect of advances;

- ☐ payments of *expenses*;

- ☐ payments by way of a *pension, allowance or gratuity* in connection with retirement or as compensation for loss of office;

---

[8] WA s.8 (5).
[9] WA s.7 (1).
[10] WA s.7 (3).
[11] WA s.7 (4).
[12] By WA s.7 (2) (a) to (e).

- payments referable to *redundancy*; and
- payments made to a worker *otherwise than in his capacity as a worker.*

Workers covered

The requirements in section 1 apply to a very much wider section of the workforce than the Truck Acts did. Specifically, "worker" means[13] for these purposes, an individual who has entered into, or works (or has worked), under:

- a contract of service; or
- a contract of apprenticeship; or
- any other type of contract requiring personal performance of any work or services.

This last category would not apply, however, to situations where the individual is running a business or profession, and the other party is his customer or client – a question which, if it arises, will be determined on the facts of each case.

The requirements also apply to employees of government departments and those carrying out functions on behalf of the Crown, and those in the National Health Service.[14] Workers on United Kingdom registered ships are included unless the employment is wholly outside the United Kingdom, they are not ordinarily resident in the United Kingdom or are working under a "crew agreement" under the Merchant Shipping Act 1970.[15] Also excluded from the requirements are members of the armed forces,[16] and those who, under their contract, ordinarily work outside Great Britain.[17] In practice,

[13] WA s.8 (1).
[14] WA s.9 (1) to (3).
[15] WA s.30 (1) to (3).
[16] WA s.9 (4).
[17] WA s.30 (1).

employees who can show they are *based* here (even though they spend a lot of time abroad) may not necessarily be excluded.[18]

Contractual and written authorisation

The reference in section 1 (1) to any *relevant provision* of the worker's contract requires consideration. What is specifically required[19] – if a deduction (or payment to the employer) is to satisfy the Act – is authority from *either*:

☐ one or more *written terms* of the contract which the employer has given the worker prior to the deduction being made, or the deduction being received; or

☐ one or more contractual terms, which can be *express or implied* (and if express, need only be orally agreed). In this case the employer is required to have previously notified the worker in writing of the existence and effect of such terms.

It is not possible for the employer to retrospectively authorise a deduction (or receipt of a payment) by obtaining a variation in the contract or written consent.[20]

Exceptions

There are a number of circumstances in which the restrictions on deductions (and payments) are specifically excluded.[21] These are where they are made:

☐ to reimburse the employer for overpayments of wages

---

[18] *Todd* v *British Midland Airways Ltd.* (1978) IRLR 370 (applying *Wilson* v *Maynard Shipbuilding Consultants* (1977) IRLR 491).
[19] WA s.1 (3); *Pename Ltd* v *Paterson* IRLIB 13.12.88.
[20] WA s.1 (4).
[21] By WA s.1 (5) (a) to (f).

or expenses (see further on overpayments page 103 above);

☐ as a result of statutory disciplinary proceedings (for example in the case of the police or fire services);

☐ to satisfy statutory payments that must be paid to a public authority;

☐ as a result of arrangements to pay sums to a third party (for example dues payable to a trade union) of an amount notified by that party as being due. The arrangements must have been established in the worker's contract (and been agreed to in writing), or have otherwise received the worker's prior consent in writing;

☐ when the worker has taken part in a "strike" or "other industrial action" – in this event the question of the employer's authority to make the deduction (or receive the payment) would depend on whether the action *did* amount to this or not (see page 91 above); and

☐ to satisfy sums due from the worker to the employer under court or tribunal orders, when this has been agreed to by the worker in writing.

What constitutes a "deduction"?

The fact that a deduction has been made may not be obvious (at first anyway) unless it is explained as such in the worker's pay statement (see page 67 above). Even if there is nothing in the pay statement, or in any other communication from the employer, the Act will treat a situation where the total wages received are less than the total that is properly payable as a deduction.[22]

If, however, the deficiency in pay is attributable to an "error of computation" it will not be treated as a deduction.[23] What is envisaged here is an error on the

[22] WA s.8 (3).
[23] WA s.8 (3).

part of the employer that affects the computation of gross wages[24] – but once the mistake is pointed out to the employer (or otherwise becomes apparent), and it is not corrected, the shortfall would clearly, it is suggested, be back within the concept of a "deduction".

If an employer claims that his method of computation of gross wages is authorised by the contract (and there is some basis for the claim), then the proper forum for deciding this would be the ordinary courts rather than the industrial tribunal (notably in an action by the employee for breach of contract and arrears of pay). A failure to pay the wages may also amount to repudiation of the contract entitling the employee to claim constructive dismissal.[25]

7.3 Retail workers

Workers covered

There are a number of *additional* restrictions which apply to workers in retail employment. For these restrictions to apply the worker need not necessarily be employed on a regular basis, but certain other points must be satisfied. Specifically, the work *must* involve:

☐ the carrying out by the worker of *retail transactions*, i.e. the sale or supply of goods, or the supply of services (including financial services); or

☐ the *collection of amounts payable* in connection with such transactions,

directly with *members of the public*, or with *fellow workers*, or other *individuals in their personal capacities*.[26]

---

[24] WA s.8 (4).
[25] *Industrial Rubber Products* v *C. Gillon* (1977) IRLR 389 at 390; *Western Excavating (ECC) Ltd.* v *Sharp* (1978) ICR 221; IRLR 27. See further pages 114 to 115.
[26] WA s.2 (1).

The last category referred to has the effect of taking workers *out* of the concept of retail employment if they deal directly with companies and corporate bodies and their representatives.

The scope of protection would therefore, at first sight seem to be wide, and extend to such diverse groups as shop assistants, cashiers (if they deal directly with the public), canteen workers, and ticket sales staff. On the other hand sizeable groups of workers who might be closely connected with retail employment (such as warehouse staff, delivery workers, kitchen personnel, etc.) may well, depending on their particular circumstances, be *outside* the definition. As trainees on government schemes like YTS (Youth Training Scheme) are not generally treated as employees they are likely to be excluded.[27]

What the restrictions are

The additional restrictions referred to are concerned with:

☐ the *amount* of pay that can be deducted because of cash shortages or stock deficiencies; and

☐ *time limits* within which deductions must be made.

There are requirements, too, which relate to *payments* received by employers on account of cash shortages and stock deficiencies.

Amounts deductible

Even if the worker's contract (or a written authorisation) permits deductions to be made (already discussed in pages 129 to 132 above) there is a limit to the amount that may be recovered on any one payday[28] of 10 per cent of

[27] *Daley* v *Allied Suppliers* (1983) IRLR 14. See, though, Ch. 2, note 18.
[28] "A day on which wages are payable to the worker"; WA s.2 (2).

the *gross wages* payable on that day.[29] In effect, therefore, employers may often have to recover shortages by instalments over successive pay days.

This restriction does *not* apply to the final instalment of wages payable to the worker.[30] This means pay referable to the last of the periods in which he is employed prior to the termination of the contract (for whatever reason) – but it is important to note that this does *not* include wages referable to any earlier periods. It would include any money paid *in lieu* of notice paid after the last wages due. It is irrelevant whether any amounts paid are paid before or after termination of the contract if they are to constitute a "final instalment of wages" and therefore be available for deduction.

Time limits on deductions

A deduction is not lawful unless it is made within twelve months of the shortage or deficiency being *established* by the employer, or the date when he *ought reasonably* to have done so.[31] In the case of a series of deductions the time limit will be satisfied if the first deduction is made within this twelve month period.

Payments

The Act renders payments to the employer (on account of shortages or deficiencies) unlawful unless several conditions are satisfied. Specifically:[32]

☐ there must have been prior written notification of the total amount owed; *and*

☐ a demand for payment that satisfies the Act in the following ways:

[29] WA s.2 (1).
[30] WA s.4 (1), (2).
[31] WA s.2 (3).
[32] WA s.3 (1).

(a) it must be in *writing* and be made on one of the worker's *pay days*;[33]

(b) a demand, as it applies to a particular shortage, must not be made earlier than the first pay day after the day on which the worker was notified of the full amount owed (or, if he is notified on a payday, that day);

(c) as with deductions, demands for payment may not be made more than twelve months after the shortage was, or ought reasonably to have been established;[34] and

(d) demands must not require more than 10 per cent of gross wages payable on the payday in question; and the payment demanded, when added to any *deductions* made, must not exceed 10 per cent of the gross wages payable.[35] The 10 per cent limit does not apply to the final instalment of wages.[36]

Notifying payment demand to employees

If the demand is to be legally effective it must either be:

☐ *given* to the worker; or

☐ *posted* to, or left at, his last known address.

This must be done either on the payday in question, or, if that is not a working day of the employer's business, on the *first working day* after that day.[37]

Legal proceedings against employees

An employer may, of course, be entitled to go to court to recover cash shortages or stock deficiencies. But he may

[33] WA s.3 (2).
[34] WA s.3 (3).
[35] WA s.3 (4).
[36] WA s.4 (3).
[37] WA s.3 (6).

not do this after the twelve month period referred to unless a demand has been served within that period. However, the court can only order repayment instalments of up to 10 per cent of gross wages (although this would *not* apply to amounts that could be paid by the worker from his final instalment of wages, or sums he could pay *after* his employment has ended).[38]

Tribunal complaints

If the requirements which have been described in the preceding paragraphs have not been observed, there is a right to bring a complaint to an industrial tribunal, and any attempt to exclude or limit this right (for example in the contract) will be ineffective.[39] The right to bring complaints because of the employer's failure to provide a proper pay statement (page 68 above) gives an employee further redress. This right is maintained by the 1986 Act, subject to the point that if an order is made under that Act *and* under the rules as to pay statements the total amount that can be ordered to be paid must not exceed the amount of the deduction.[40]

The rules governing the bringing of complaints are contained in section 5 of the Act. The main ones are that complaints must be brought within three months of the deduction being made (or payment received) – in the case of a series of deductions or payments the date of the last one in the series is taken. Complaints brought outside these limits may nevertheless be considered if it was not reasonably practicable to comply with them.

The tribunal, if it upholds the complaint, must make a declaration to that effect and order the employer to pay the worker the amount of any deduction (or payment) unlawfully made (or received). And payments or repayments already made to the worker are discounted.

[38] WA s.4 (4), (5).
[39] WA s.6 (1), (3).
[40] WA s.6 (2).

When a complaint is made to a tribunal this fact will be notified to the conciliation service (ACAS). In any case, the parties can ask ACAS to try to reach a conciliated agreement, and the arrangements for conciliating disputes have been applied to problems arising under the Wages Act 1986.[41] Agreements can be made following a conciliation officer's intervention which provide for a complaint not to be brought (or to be discontinued), and these can be treated as legally effective.[42]

Dismissal of employees

The restrictions which the 1986 Act place on employers of retail staff might, in some circumstances, prompt them to dismiss the worker concerned and thereupon make unlimited deductions (or demands for payments) on termination, as the Act appears to permit them to do (pages 135 to 136 above) – thus imposing what has been described as a "double indemnity".[43] The Act contains no anti-avoidance provisions to deal with this eventuality, although there may be scope (for workers who have the necessary length of service, etc.) for compensation if a successful unfair dismissal claim can be brought.

However, the fact that a deduction may be unlawful, or unauthorised by the contract, may not, in itself, prevent an employer being able to properly dismiss an employee if what the employer is really relying on is misconduct, or some other reason entitling the employer to dismiss. Cases illustrating this point also show how, despite regulatory legislation, an employer retains the dismissal sanction to reinforce instructions as to working methods, calculation of piece-work rates, etc. Thus in *Chell* v *Hall and Boardman*[44] miners were paid by the

---
[41] EPCA s.133, as amended by WA s.32(1), Sch. 4, para. 9.
[42] WA s.6 (3).
[43] Painter and Leighton *The Wages Act: A Critical Guide* in *Employee Relations* (1986) Vol. 8 No. 6 at p. 27.
[44] (1896) 12 TLR 408; Freedland p. 220.

weight of minerals obtained. Deductions were banned by section 12 of the Coal Mines Regulation Act 1887. They had been warned though, not to allow dust into the tubs used to measure the coal, and a dismissal for doing this was held to be justified for disobedience to orders.

There might be circumstances where deductions, etc., indicate that an employer is attempting to *vary* the contract of employment. This may be the case, for example, where the employer, in making the deduction is effectively trying to introduce a power to quantify or reduce wages which was not previously included in the contract. In this event there may be scope for treating such conduct as a breach of the contract entitling the employee to sue for damages including any shortfall in wages due[45] or, possibly, as a repudiation of the contract entitling the employee to treat the contract as at an end and complain of constructive dismissal (see, further, the cases discussed in Chapter 6 above).

In the absence of a contractual right to make deductions or require payments it is not appropriate to give an employee a "choice" of either "accepting" a deduction or being dismissed. Thus in *D. V. Lethaby* v *Horsman Andrew and Knill Ltd.*,[46] a coal merchant's delivery man failed to deliver the correct amount of coal to a customer. There was insufficient evidence to suggest dishonesty on the delivery-man's part, and there was no contractual right to make deductions. He was told that he must accept a deduction (intended to be the equivalent of the price of the coal) or face dismissal. After the deduction was made, and the applicant had left the employment, he was able to successfully claim for unfair dismissal.

---

[45] *Rigby* v *Ferodo Ltd.* (1987) IRLR 516, H.L.
[46] (1975) IRLR 119.

7.4 Court orders

Attachment of Earnings Act 1971

Employers may be obliged to made deductions from an employee's pay (and possibly pension) as a result of an "attachment of earnings" order made under this Act. This can be used to secure payment by the employee (or "debtor" as he is referred to) of payments due under maintenance orders, judgement debts, fines and certain other court orders. A court making attachment of earnings orders can require information about earnings, anticipated earnings, resources and needs, etc., to be provided by a debtor; and details of earnings and anticipated earnings to be provided by anybody appearing to employ him.[47] Employers and debtors are subject to criminal penalties for non-compliance.

Scheme of the Act

An order operates as an instruction to a specified person "who appears to the court to have the debtor in his employment", section 6 (1) – note that it is *not* an order which can be directed at persons *generally* who might be the debtor's employer nor can it be made against parties like agents who might make payments to an employee, section 6 (2). The employer must make periodical deductions from the debtor's "earnings", as defined by section 24 (see page 143 below), in accordance with the Act and in amounts and at times laid down by the order or as allowed by the court. Payments are made to a collecting officer.

The key parts of an order are, for deduction purposes:

☐ *the normal deduction rate*, i.e. the deduction per week, month, etc., which the court thinks reasonable; and

☐ the *protected earnings rate*, i.e. the rate below which,

---

[47] Attachment of Earnings Act 1971, s.14.

having regard to the debtor's resources and needs, the court thinks it reasonable that the earnings paid to him should not be reduced. In practice this means a level which should not normally be below "subsistence level" by reference to the Social Security scale rates in force.[48]

Both these points must be clearly specified.[49]

Specific requirements

The employer must comply with orders addressed to him, although he will not be liable for non-compliance until seven days after its service (section 7 (1)). He must inform the court if the debtor is not in his employment, or has left it.[50] If a person becomes the debtor's employer, and is aware of an order (and the court that made it) he is obliged to notify the court of this fact, and provide a written notification of the debtor's earnings, or anticipated earnings; there are corresponding obligations on the debtor to give notice of job changes, and to provide details of his earnings to the court.[51]

There are various circumstances in which an order may either cease to have effect (e.g. on an order of commitment being made, or registration of a maintenance order),[52] or may be discharged.[53] In this event, or when further compliance with an order is not required because all payments due have been paid, notice is given to the employer under section 12. The obligation to make deductions thereupon ceases. There is also a seven day "period of grace" following service of the discharging order during which there is no liability should the order be treated as still in force.

[48] *Billington* v *Billington* (1974) 1 All E.R. 546.
[49] s.6. (5).
[50] s.7 (2).
[51] s.15.
[52] s.9.
[53] ss.8, 11.

A written statement of the total amount deducted must be provided to the debtor every time a deduction is made, and that amount may include fifty pence[54] to cover the employer's clerical and administrative costs.[55]

Making deductions

Detailed rules governing deductions are in the Schedules to the Act. Before looking at the main ones, in Schedule 3, it is necessary to note the meaning of two expressions commonly used in the legislation. One is "earnings", and the other is "attachable earnings".

For the general purposes of the Act "earnings" means[56] sums payable by way of:

☐ wages or salary – and this would specifically include fees, bonus payments, commission, overtime pay, or any other emoluments paid in addition to wages or salary, or paid under a contract of service;

☐ pension (including annuities for past services, and payments for loss, diminution, etc., or office); and

☐ Statutory Sick Pay.

A number of payments are excluded by section 24 (2), the most important of which are the guaranteed minimum state pension, disablement or disability pension or allowances,[57] and certain social security payments. If an employer, debtor or creditor wishes, he can obtain a ruling by the court as to whether particular payments constitute "earnings" – there is no liability for not making deductions while that is done.[58]

"Attachable earnings" are earnings which are payable

---

[54] SI 1980 No. 558.
[55] s.7 (4).
[56] s.24 (1).
[57] In *Miles* v *Miles* (1979) 1 All E.R. 865, an "ill-health" pension calculated by reference to length of service, and not the extent of disability, was *not* excluded.
[58] s.16.

to a debtor on any payday *after* deduction of income tax, Class 1 contributions and amounts deductible under other legislation or for certain superannuation schemes (Sch. 3, para. 3).

On a payday on which attachable earnings exceed the debtor's protected earnings the employer must:[59]

☐ make the normal deduction, i.e. the amount specified in the order for the relevant period; and

☐ also deduct any arrears which have not been deducted from previous paydays when the full deduction has not been possible.

In no circumstances can deductions be made when attachable earnings are equal to or less than the protected earnings level (page 141 above), although the shortfall will be carried forward to future paydays when earnings *will* be adequate.

There are detailed rules governing the priority which must be given where there are two or more orders applicable to the same debtor.[60] Broadly, with orders which do not secure sums under an administration order, they must be dealt with in the order in which they are made. After the first one is dealt with, any balance left over (after protected earnings are paid over) can be applied to later orders. Orders in respect of judgement debts and administration orders have less priority than other types.

7.5 Tax and National Insurance

Pay As You Earn (PAYE)

Income tax under Schedule E is charged on the emoluments of the current tax year. It is collected by a method

[59] Sch. 3, paras. 1 to 6.
[60] For a detailed guide to the operation of PAYE see the Inland Revenue booklet *Employer's Guide to PAYE* (P7) available free from any tax office.

of deduction at source by the employer known as the PAYE system and *must* be applied to all employees[61] earning more than a defined limit – usually the weekly equivalent of the single person's allowance for income tax. For the so-called "higher paid" employees (including directors) the employer must also complete a form P.11D giving details of benefits in kind and payments by way of expenses. The PAYE system is an effective form of collection of tax which removes much of the opportunity for tax evasion[62] by employees. After deduction of tax under the PAYE scheme the employer must pay it over to the Collector of Taxes within fourteen days of the end of each tax month.

Each employee is issued with a code number by his tax office which varies having regard to the amount of allowances available to the employee.[63] The employer then operates a deductions working sheet for each employee which, along with tax tables provided by the Inland Revenue, determines the amount of tax to be deducted from the employee's wages. Employee's contributions to an approved pension scheme are deducted from his gross pay before calculation of tax. In theory, the income tax liability of each employee on his taxable emoluments should, as far as possible, be satisfied by the deductions made under this system.

At the end of each tax year, the employer must give each of his employees a form P.60 giving details including gross taxable emoluments, income tax deducted and code number. This enables employees to check the correctness of the deductions and make a claim to the

---

[61] This system is also applied to workers who are supplied by agencies (see Chapter 2) and similar rules apply to self-employed workers in the construction industry unless they can produce a tax exemption certificate. Note that the tax office may exempt the employer from the necessity to deduct tax at source in certain circumstances, for example students who are unlikely to earn more than their personal relief threshold in a tax year.
[62] I.e. non declaration of taxable income.
[63] E.g. if male, whether he is married or single.

Inland Revenue direct for any adjustment. At the same time the employer must forward to the Collector of Taxes a certificate for each employee (P.14) containing similar information.

There are special rules for employees joining or leaving the employment during the tax year. Every employee who leaves the employment or is dismissed must be handed a tax form P.45 by the employer which shows cumulative pay to date and the tax deducted therefrom. The employee should then hand this over to any new employer who will then operate the PAYE system from these cumulative totals.

National Insurance contributions[64]

Both the employer and employee are liable to pay Class 1 National Insurance contributions at appropriate rates on payments classed as earnings for these purposes. Though a detailed explanation is outside the scope of the book, briefly, most of the benefits discussed in Chapter 2 are excluded from the definition of "earnings" with the exception of the employee's contributions to any pension scheme. Although deductible for tax purposes such contributions are not deductible for National Insurance purposes and consideration should be given by the employer to reducing the level of employee's salary and instead making the pension scheme non-contributory. This has the advantage of saving both employer's and employee's contributions on the amount of the contribution to the pension scheme formerly paid by the employee.

The employee's contributions (payable on a graduated scale up to a maximum of 9 per cent on wages up to £305 per week) must be deducted at source by the employer alongside the PAYE deduction. The employer's contribution at 10.45 per cent of the employee's earnings

---

[64] For a detailed summary see the DHSS booklet *Employer's Guide to National Insurance* (NP 15).

(without any upper limit) is effectively a payroll tax though is fully deductible for income tax purposes.

7.6 Deducting union subscriptions

It is quite common for a union, usually at company level, to agree an arrangement with an employer – known as "check-off" – whereby the employer deducts subscriptions from its members' pay and then pays the amounts over to the union. The company's authority for doing this, for the purpose of satisfying the requirements of the Wages Act 1986 (see page 129 above), is usually obtained from:

☐ authorisation in the individual's contract, or else a provision in a collective agreement dealing with deductions (which may be incorporated in the member's individual contract); and

☐ the individual member providing other written authority for the deduction.

A requirement to belong to a union (where that union operates a "closed shop" arrangement with the employer[65]) will often be accompanied by such an arrangement; but in any case it may be a facility operated for union members.

Withdrawing authority to deduct

It was not always clear, especially when a closed shop was operating, at what point an employee was entitled to require the employer to stop making union deductions.[66] Since the relevant provisions of the Employment Act 1988[67] came into force an employer *must* stop deduc-

---

[65] Although closed shops have not been abolished, they have been severely curtailed by EA ss.10 and 11.
[66] As in *Sakals* v *United Counties Omnibus Co. Ltd* (1984) IRLR 474, EAT.

tions once an employee certifies to him that membership of the union has ended (or will end) on a particular date; or that notice to the union terminating membership has expired (or will expire) on a particular date. The requirement to stop deductions will only operate, however, from the first day when it becomes reasonably practicable to comply with the employee's certificate. Note that breaches of these rules will amount to an unlawful deduction under the Wages Act 1986, section 1(1) (as to which see p.129 above).

If pressure is imposed on staff to pay union dues, payments in lieu of such dues, etc, this can constitute "action short of dismissal", and could become the subject of an industrial tribunal complaint: dismissal of employees because of their objection to paying dues or other payments (or otherwise in connection with their refusal to be in union membership) will generally be treated as unfair.[68]

Political levy; "contracting out"

Under the Trade Union Act 1913[69] a member has the right to be exempted from paying a political levy if the union has a political fund. As far as check-off arrangements are concerned an employer must ensure[70] that no amount representing a contribution to the fund is deducted if the individual concerned has provided written notification to him that he has:

☐ been *exempted* from contributions; or

☐ notified the union under the 1913 Act that he objects to contributions.

This obligation only applies, though, from when it

---

[67] EA s.7 (1) to (3).
[68] EPCA ss.23 and 58, as amended.
[69] As amended by the Trade Union Act 1984.
[70] Trade Union Act 1984, s.18 (1).

becomes reasonably practicable to comply with the notification.[71]

Because of the extra administrative cost of making arrangements for staff who have "contracted out" of paying political levy, or for other reasons, an employer may refuse to operate check-off for such staff. This can contravene the 1984 Act, though, if ordinary check-off arrangements are still operating for other employees.[72]

Staff can apply for court orders to stop deductions of political levy (or to require check-off without the inclusion of political levy to carry on).[73]

---

[71] *Ibid*, s.18 (2).
[72] *Ibid*, s.18 (3).
[73] *Ibid* s.18 (4), (5).

Chapter 8

TERMINATION AND WAGES PROBLEMS

In this chapter the obligations of an employer on termination to pay wages or make other payments (such as payments to compensate for loss of earnings on unfair dismissal etc.) are considered. Specifically, the following matters are dealt with:

☐ voluntary termination;

☐ dismissal;

☐ the employer's insolvency;

☐ the transfer of the undertaking;

☐ frustration of the contract; and

☐ taxation of terminal payments.

8.1 Voluntary termination

In most cases the employee's contract will end when he decides to leave, or it is otherwise mutually agreed that he is leaving voluntarily, and the obligation to pay wages will cease at that time.

Employees are required to give notice that they are leaving[1] and are entitled to receive minimum periods of notice (see page 153 below). Periods that are longer than the statutory minimum periods can be put into the contract. If the employee works out his notice period, he must be paid his normal wages during that time, it may be convenient, however, for the employer if the

---

[1] One week if they have been continuously employed for one month or more; EPCA s.49 (2).

employee leaves before the expiry of his notice period. This can be arranged but the employee is still entitled to be paid for the unworked notice period.[2] The employee can waive his right to receive notice (and his right to wages during the notice period), for example, if he needs to leave immediately to take another job.

There are two further situations which require consideration. Firstly, where an employee is employed on a *fixed-term contract*; and secondly, when it has been agreed that the job will only last for as long as it will take to complete a *specified task*.

Fixed-term contracts

Where the employment contract is expressed to last for a fixed period of time, the lapse of such a contract without renewal is deemed to be a *dismissal* for the purposes of unfair dismissal and redundancy payment claims. However, an employee whose contract is for a fixed-term of two years or more may agree in writing to *waive* redundancy payment and unfair dismissal claims (section 142, EPCA). It should be noted that a contract is still a "fixed-term" contract even if it contains a clause allowing for earlier termination during its currency.[3]

Contracts for a specific task; automatic termination

In *Wiltshire County Council* v *NATFHE and Guy*[4] the Court of Appeal distinguished between a fixed-term contract and a contract for the completion of a particular task. In the latter case there is no "dismissal". Such a contract is discharged by performance and so a claim for unfair dismissal or redundancy payments is excluded. More recently, it has also been decided that there is no dismissal in the case of contracts which are terminable

---

[2] EPCA s.49 (3).
[3] See *BBC* v *Dixon* (1979) IRLR 114 C.A.
[4] (1980) IRLR 198.

on the happening or non-happening of a particular event.

☐ *Example*
A lecturer's contract, was expressed to last "only so long as sufficient funds are provided by the Manpower Services Commission or by other firms or sponsors". It was held to have automatically terminated when the MSC withdrew its funding. As a result there was no dismissal for redundancy.[5]

An additional problem has arisen in cases where the employer and employee agree that the contract will terminate automatically if the employee fails to fulfil a certain condition e.g. return to work on a given date following a period of extended leave. If valid, such agreements would mean that the contract ends by *mutual agreement* rather than by dismissal and thus prevents a claim for unfair dismissal and/or redundancy payments. It is now clear that these "automatic termination" agreements are void under EPCA section 140.[6] This section makes void any arrangement or agreement which purports to "exclude or limit" employment rights.

This is not to say that termination by mutual consent can never succeed. If the employee is genuinely willing to leave, then section 140 will not invalidate the agreement. This is important in the wages context because a termination may well be agreed to by an employee in return for financial compensation or under an early retirement scheme. In this case the contract can be treated as terminated by mutual consent.[7]

---

[5] *Brown and others* v *Knowsley Borough Council* (1986) IRLR 102 EAT.
[6] *Igbo* v *Johnson Matthey Chemicals Ltd.* (1986) IRLR 215.
[7] *Birch & Humber* v *University of Liverpool* (1985) IRLR 165.

8.2 Dismissal

Dismissal by notice

A contract of employment can be terminated on the giving of notice if this is something which has been specifically agreed by the parties. In the absence of an expressly-agreed notice period, the law will imply a period of "reasonable notice" whose length will depend on the circumstances of the employment, including the intervals at which wages are payable (e.g. weekly or monthly).

Statute has now intervened in order to require the following minimum periods of notice:

☐ one week for an employee continuously employed for more than one month but less than two years;

☐ one week for each year of continuous employment, for an employee employed for two years or more but less than twelve years; and

☐ twelve weeks for an employee employed for twelve years or more.[8]

The employer may pay the employee wages in lieu of notice, but cannot contract out of the obligation to either provide (or pay for) the relevant statutory minimum period.

Guaranteed earnings during notice

The EPCA guarantees an employee's income during the statutory minimum notice period. The detailed rules are set out in Schedule 3 to the Act but may be summarised as follows:

(a) the employee is entitled to a normal week's pay during the notice period even though they do no not work, if:

[8] EPCA s.49.

- [ ] he is ready and willing to work but the employer can provide no work; or
- [ ] he is incapable of work through sickness or injury; or
- [ ] he is away on a contractually agreed holiday;[9]

(b) any sickness or industrial injury benefit claimed during the notice period may be deducted in calculating the employee's entitlement, and the right to payment will be excluded completely where:

- [ ] the employee takes time off (including time off governed by statute such as that allowed to carry out trade union duties, to perform certain public duties, to look for work or to receive ante-natal care);[10]
- [ ] the employee breaks the contract during the period of notice and is rightfully summarily dismissed; and
- [ ] the employee has given notice but then goes on strike.[11]

Where the employer terminates the contract by giving shorter notice than is expressly or implicitly provided for, the employee will be entitled to bring an action for wrongful dismissal in the county court or High Court. The damages recoverable will amount to a sum representing the wages payable had the employee been allowed to work out the correct period of notice. Where the employer has paid the full wages entitlement in lieu of notice, an employer may still be liable for further damages if the premature termination of the contract has prevented the employee attaining the requisite continuity of employment necessary to claim unfair dismissal and other statutory rights.[12]

---

[9] Schedule 3, paras. 2 and 3.
[10] See pages 99 to 103 above.
[11] Schedule 3, paras. 5, 6 and 7.
[12] See the views expressed in *Robert Cort & Son Ltd.* v *Charman* (1981) ICR 816, and *Stapp* v *The Shaftesbury Society* (1982) IRLR 326.

Dismissal without notice

At common law, an employer is entitled to dismiss an employee *summarily* (i.e. without notice or wages in lieu of notice) if the employee has broken an essential term of the contract.[13] In such a situation, both parties are immediately released from any future obligations under the contract. However, certain past obligations will survive such as the obligation to pay the dismissed employee any accrued holiday or back pay and to reimburse any outstanding expenses.

If the employer fails to dismiss for good cause, the employee may bring an action for wrongful dismissal.[14] As stated earlier, the damages recoverable will generally only compensate the employee for the wages s/he would have received had lawful notice been given.[15] The employee will be unable to recover damages for the humiliating manner of the dismissal or for loss of reputation leading to future difficulty in obtaining employment.

Furthermore, the law will only take into account the employer's definite wage liabilities in calculating damages: it will ignore those financial rewards which are within the employer's discretion to make and from which the employee might have benefited had they worked out their notice period.

---

[13] See *Wilson* v *Racher* (1974) ICR 428; and generally, Bowers pp. 137 to 138.

[14] See, generally, Bowers ch. 9; Smith and Wood, ch. 5.

[15] *Addis* v *Gramophone Company Ltd.* (1909) A.C. 488; *Bliss* v *South East Thames RHA* (1985) IRLR 308. Certain exceptional contracts have been held to have envisaged a reward to the employee over and above wages and the damage awards have reflected this additional loss, e.g. the loss of publicity where an acting engagement was cancelled (*Marbe* v *George Edwards (Daly's Theatres) Ltd.* (1928) 1 K.B. 269); the diminution of future employment prospects where a contract of apprenticeship was broken (*Dunk v George Waller and Son Ltd.* (1970) 2 All E.R. 630).

☐ *Example*
An employee who was wrongfully dismissed had been employed on a five year contract with a salary which was subject to certain periodic discretionary bonuses. After he had been dismissed, but during the period in which the contract should have continued, the employers discontinued the bonus scheme and increased the wages of their staff.

The majority decision of the Court of Appeal was that the increase in wages should not be taken into account when calculating damages, since the only contractual placed duty upon the employers was to pay the fixed salary and anything on top of that was discretionary.[16]

Given the restrictive nature of these rules, the action for damages for wrongful dismissal, for most employees, is hardly worth the trouble and expense of bringing it to court. It may be a worthwhile option, however, in the case of a highly paid employee either employed on a fixed-term contract with no provision for earlier termination or entitled under the contract to a substantial period of notice.

In the modern context, most employees would be better advised to look towards the statutory remedies of unfair dismissal or redundancy payments should they wish to claim compensation for their dismissal.

The EPCA defines the following events as dismissals for unfair dismissal and redundancy payment purposes:

☐ termination of the contract with or without notice by the employer (section 55 (2) (a) and section 83 (2) (a));

☐ the lapse of a fixed-term contract without renewal (section 55 (2) (b) and section 83 (2) (b)); and

☐ the termination of the contract by the employee as a result of a serious breach of contract by the employer ("constructive dismissal": section 55 (2) (c) and section 83 (2) (c)).

[16] *Lavarack* v *Woods of Colchester Ltd.* (1966) 3 All E.R. 683.

If dismissal of the employee is held to be unfair in all the circumstances, the employee is entitled to compensation calculated in the following way. The *basic award* is an award of half, one, or one and a half weeks' pay for each year of continuous service (depending on age), subject to a maximum of twenty years. The maximum allowable for a week's pay is currently £164: this figure is reviewed each year and any changes made operate from April 1.

If Aged	But Less Than	No. Of Weeks' Pay For Each Year
—	22	½
22	41	1
41	65	1½

N.B. If the applicant is aged 64, entitlement goes down by one twelfth for each month after the 64th birthday.

Therefore, the maximum payment under this head of calculation in the year 1988/89 will be:

☐ £164 x 20 x 1½ = £4920

Note that where the principal reason for the dismissal is that of redundancy, the employee's statutory entitlement will also be calculated in this way. However, those who successfully claim unfair dismissal may also be entitled to a *compensatory award*. This is an amount which the industrial tribunal considers just and equitable. The maximum here in 1988/89 will be £8500.

In unfair dismissal claims both heads of compensation may be reduced if the applicant contributed to his dismissal or as a result of any conduct before dismissal.

An *additional award* may be made where an order for reinstatement or re-engagement is not complied with. If the original reason for the dismissal was for a reason other than sex, race or trade union discrimination, the award may be between thirteen and twenty-six weeks' pay. If the reason was for discrimination, then there is a discretion to award between twenty-six and fifty-two weeks' pay.

8.3 The employer's insolvency

In the event of an employer's insolvency, certain debts owed by an employer to an employee are treated as *preferential debts*.[17] In other words, the employee's claims will be paid out from what remains of the employer's funds, along with outstanding PAYE tax and VAT contributions, before the claims of ordinary creditors.

The preferential creditor status of employees is, however, restricted to the following payments:

☐ any "wages accrued" during the four months before the date of insolvency, subject to a maximum of £800. "Wages" in this context are defined to include remuneration in respect of holidays, sick pay and accrued holiday remuneration and commission payments;

☐ a guarantee payment;

☐ a medical suspension payment;

☐ payment for time off for trade union duties, to look for alternative employment or for antenatal care; and;

☐ a protective award for failure to consult over redundancies.

Every employee's claim for the payments set out above ranks equally, and, if the assets are insufficient for the claim to be paid in full, will be settled on a pro rata basis.

Additional protection

An additional protection is provided by the EPCA which gives an employee the right to recover certain

[17] EPCA s.122.

payments owed to him/her by the insolvent employer from the government-administered Redundancy Fund. These payments include:

- □ up to eight weeks' arrears of wages, including quarantee pay, medical suspension pay, any payment for time off for trade union duties, to seek alternative employment when under notice of redundancy or for antenatal care, Statutory Sick Pay and any protective award;
- □ wages during the statutory minimum notice period;
- □ up to six weeks' accrued holiday pay;
- □ any basic award for compensation for unfair dismissal;
- □ reimbursement of premiums or fees paid for apprenticeship or articles of clerkship; and
- □ any statutory redundancy or maternity payment.

Where any of the sums listed above is calculated by reference to weekly pay, the maximum amount that can be taken into account is currently £164 per week (section 122 (5)). The Secretary of State reviews this figure each year (section 122 (6) and section 148). The figure refers to gross – as opposed to take-home – pay.[18]

These payments are subject to a reduction if the employee earns money elsewhere or receives unemployment or other social security benefits during what should have been his or her notice period. In the case of the long-term unemployed, deducting unemployment benefit during the notice period would leave them worse off than if they had been given proper notice because they would not receive the full financial advantage of their one year entitlement to unemployment benefit.

Following protracted litigation,[19] the position has

[18] See *Morris* v *Secretary of State for Employment* (1985) IRLR 297.
[19] See *Westwood* v *Secretary of State for Employment* (1984) IRLR 209 H.L.

now been clarified by amendments to the legislation concerned.[20] As a result, the former employee receives the insolvency payment (less the amount received as unemployment benefit) but can still, if necessary, have a further full one year's benefit.

Unpaid employer contributions to pension schemes

The trustees of an occupational pension scheme may claim such arrears from the Redundancy Fund. The sum payable is the *least* of the following amounts:

☐ arrears accrued within the twelve months prior to the insolvency;

☐ arrears certified by an actuary to be necessary to pay the employee's benefits on dissolution of the scheme;

☐ 10 per cent of the last twelve months' total pay of all the employees covered by the scheme.

How to claim arrears of wages etc from the redundancy fund

Written requests for payment should be made to the Department of Employment. The liquidator or receiver is under a statutory duty to supply a statement to the Secretary of State certifying the amount of the arrears. The Secretary of State will then make a payment. Where it appears to the Secretary of State that there is likely to be an unreasonable delay in obtaining this statement, payment may be made without its receipt.

Where a payment from the fund is made, any of the employee's rights and remedies in respect of that debt against the employer are transferred to the Secretary of State. Disputes concerning an employee's entitlement to reimbursement from the Redundancy Fund are handled by industrial tribunals.

---

[20] The Social Security (General Benefit) Amendment Regulations 1984 (S.I. 1984 No. 1259).

8.4 The transfer of the undertaking

At common law, an employee could not be transferred without his or her consent from one employer to another.[21] This rule was explicable on the basis of freedom of contract. This "freedom", however, could work against employees because, equally, the employer was under no obligation to employ existing employees who worked in the transferred business.

Under the EPCA, until 1981, if an employee who was employed at the time of the transfer was in fact re-engaged by the transferee employer, then statutory continuity was preserved for the purposes of claiming unfair dismissal, redundancy payments and the like. But the principle remained that the employer was under no obligation to offer either to renew the contracts or to re-engage in suitable alternative employment. If no such offer was made by the incoming employer, the employee was left with no alternative but to claim redundancy payments from the transferor employer.

Important changes were brought about by the Transfer of Undertakings (Protection of Employment) Regulations 1981. Now, where there is a "relevant transfer" of an undertaking from A to B:

☐ workers employed by A "immediately before the transfer" automatically have their contracts of employment transferred to B. So, for example, if a worker is entitled to a weekly wage of £200 for a thirty-seven hour week when employed by Company A, these terms will continue to bind Company B when the undertaking is transferred;

☐ B will also assume all A's rights and liabilities in relation to those employees employed "immediately before the transfer". For example, the liability for any debts owed by A to its workforce will be transferred to B;

[21] *Nokes* v *Doncaster Amalgamated Collieries Ltd.* (1940) A.C. 1014.

- □ any rights or duties arising under a collective agreement made by A with a recognised trade union continue. This is, however, expressly stated to be without prejudice to the statutory presumption that collective agreements are not intended to be legally enforceable;
- □ B is obliged to honour any union recognition agreements made by A but only "where after a relevant transfer the undertaking or part of the undertaking maintains an identity distinct from the remainder of the transferee's undertaking";
- □ A is subject to similar obligations to consult recognised trade unions over transfers of undertakings as over redundancies;
- □ dismissal of any employee by A or B for a reason connected with the transfer is deemed to be automatically unfair. This position may be modified if the dismissal was for an "economic, technical or organisational reason entailing changes in the workforce of either the transferor or the transferee before or after the relevant transfer". In this situation the dismissal will be held to be fair if it was reasonable in the circumstances.

Operation of the Transfer Regulations

The Regulations only operate if certain conditions are satisfied. Firstly, that the form of change of ownership of the undertaking falls within the scope of the Regulations. An "undertaking" is defined to include "any trade or business but does not include any undertaking or part of an undertaking which is not in the nature of a commercial venture". It would appear that a *mere transfer of assets* which falls short of a transfer of the business as a going concern, will fall outside the regulations.

Where there is a mere transfer of assets, the workers involved will not maintain statutory continuity of employment, and would be well-advised to seek redundancy payments from their former employer.

It should also be noted that the regulations do not apply to the commonest form of takeovers: a transfer of shares from Company A to Company B. This is because in this situation the identity of the employer in law remains the same and the contracts and continuity of employment of the workforce are maintained.

Secondly, automatic transfer of contracts of employment and other rights and liabilities will only cover those employees employed in the undertaking "immediately before the transfer". After a period of uncertainty, it has now been determined that only when employees are employed *at the very moment* of a business transfer does the purchaser take over the vendor's rights and liabilities in connection with the employment contracts.[22] So, for example, a business purchaser cannot be made liable for dismissals carried out by the vendor before transfer.

Finally, it is important to note that rights and liabilities over or in relation to occupational pension schemes are not automatically assigned under the Regulations.

8.5 Frustration of the contract

"Frustration" is a legal concept which, if it applies, brings the employment contract automatically to an end. As a result, there is no liability to continue paying wages, or to pay compensation for unfair dismissal, redundancy, etc.

In order for the doctrine of frustration to apply, there are two essential factors which must be present:

☐ there must be some event, not foreseen or provided for by the parties to the contract at the time it was made, which either makes it *impossible for the contract to be performed* at all, or at least renders its performance something *radically different from what the parties envisaged* when they made the contract; and

---

[22] *Secretary of State for Employment* v *Spence and others* (1986) IRLR 248.

- [ ] the event must have occurred without the fault of either contracting party. Frustration will not operate if it was "self-induced" or caused by the fault of a party.[23]

Events which have been held to frustrate the contract include the following:

- [ ] the conscription of the employee to national service;[24]
- [ ] internment as an enemy alien during wartime.[25]

However, frustration arguments have been more frequently employed in the cases of long-term absence through sickness or through imprisonment. On sickness absence: a number of factors will generally be relevant in deciding whether a contract is frustrated. These include:

(a) the terms of the contract, including any provision for sick pay;

(b) how long the employment is likely to last in the absence of sickness;

(c) whether the employee holds a "key position";

(d) the nature of the illness and how long it has already continued, and the prospects of recovery; and

(e) the period of past employment.[26]

A case recently decided provides a good illustration of the operation of the frustration doctrine:

- [ ] *Example*

    Mr. Notcutt had been employed by the same rela-

---

[23] This definition is taken from the speech of Lord Brandon in *Paal Wilson & Co. A/S v Partenreederei Hannah Blumenthal* (1983) 1 A.C. 854 at p. 909.
[24] *Morgan v Manser* (1948) 1 K.B. 184.
[25] *Unger v Preston Corporation* (1942) 1 All E.R. 200.
[26] See *Marshall v Harland & Wolff Ltd.* (1972) ICR 101; and *Egg Stores (Stamford Hill) Ltd. v Leibovici* (1977) ICR 260.

tively small company as a skilled workman for some twenty-seven years. In October 1983, when two years from retirement age, he suffered a coronary and was thereafter off work. His employer's for a time subcontracted his work on a temporary basis, but this was not wholly satisfactory, and by July 1984, decided to take on someone else if Mr. Notcutt was not going to return to work. With Mr. Notcutt's permission, the employers sought a medical report from his G.P. In that report, the doctor said that he doubted whether Mr. Notcutt would ever work again. As a result Mr. Notcutt was given twelve weeks' notice of dismissal.

Mr. Notcutt took legal advice and was informed that under EPCA he was entitled to sick pay during the notice period, notwithstanding that ordinarily under his contract he was not paid when off sick. As we have seen above, this was correct legal advice. He lodged a claim to that effect in the county court.

Ultimately, the Court of Appeal decided that the county court judge was correct in finding that Mr. Notcutt's contract of employment had been frustrated by an illness which would have probably prevented him from working again. The contract, therefore, was not terminated by the employers and Mr. Notcutt was not entitled to sick pay during the notice period.[27]

In the past imprisonment was thought to be "self-induced" frustration.[28] More recently, however, the Court of Appeal have ruled that a custodial sentence of six months *does* have the effect of frustrating the contract. It was felt that it was the sentence passed by the trial judge – as opposed to the employee's criminal conduct – which was the frustrating event. Consequently this was not a case of self-induced frustration.[29]

---

[27] *Notcutt* v *Universal Equipment Co. (London) Ltd.* (1986) IRLR 218.
[28] *Norris* v *Southampton City Council* (1982) IRLR 141.
[29] *F. C. Shepherd & Co. Ltd.* v *Jerrom* (1986) IRLR 358.

The effects of a finding of frustration

As we have seen above, frustration means there has been no "dismissal". This has a particularly serious effect on certain statutory rights to compensation and pay such as unfair dismissal, redundancy payments, and pay during the notice period.

If the contract is frustrated, the worker loses the right to further remuneration from the moment the event occurs. However, the value of any work done up to the date of frustration may be claimed under the Law Reform (Frustrated Contracts) Act, 1943. This allows the court to order the payment of a "just" amount in respect of services to which the employer has had the benefit prior to the frustrating event.

8.6 Taxation of terminal payments

From the employee's viewpoint

Whether or not any payments or benefits received by an employee on the ending of his employment are taxable depends upon the type of payment in question. There are three main types:

(a) *Contractual entitlements* – if the contract of employment expressly allows the employer to dismiss the employee with wages in lieu of notice, the payment will normally be regarded as an "emolument" and be subject to tax under the PAYE system. A similar tax treatment is accorded to lump sum payments to which the employee is entitled under his contract in the event of termination by the employer.[30]

(b) *Compensation payments* – on the other hand, termination payments such as on redundancy, or payments

---

[30] *Dale* v *De Soissons* (1950) 2 All E.R. 460.

which are regarded as damages or compensation[31] for dismissal are subject to special rules. Normally, in order to be taxable under Schedule E (outlined in Chapter 2 above), the payments made by the employer must be in the nature of a reward for services, whether past, present or future. Clearly, payments within this section would not be regarded as "rewards" and for this reason there are special provisions in the ICTA[32] to cover such payments and "golden handshakes". Briefly, any payments made on the termination of a contract of employment, whether in cash or in kind, are taxable. Employees cannot escape tax by directing payment to members of their family, nor can they obtain a tax benefit by requesting a payment in kind – such as the transfer of their company car – all are caught by the legislation. There is however a measure of relief for the employees in question as the first £30000 is exempt from tax, the balance being treated as income of the year of receipt and taxed in the normal way.

(c) *Restrictive covenants* – payments for a restrictive covenant given by the employee, for example, a promise not to work for a competitor for a certain period, were until 9 June 1988 tax free if the employee was a basic rate taxpayer. From this date however, section 73 of the Finance Act 1988 provides that such payments are now regarded as emoluments taxable under Schedule E in the year of receipt.

A global payment to an employee may be made up of

---

[31] It should be noted that in assessing the amount of compensation, the court will attempt to put the employee in the same position he would have been in had the employer not broken the contract. If the employee had been allowed to continue performing the contract he would have received his emoluments net of tax and National Insurance contributions. Damages will therefore be computed by reference to this net sum (*British Transport Commission* v *Gourley* (1956) A.C. 185).
[32] s.148.

elements from each category and must be apportioned to ascertain the overall tax liability. It is clear there is scope for tax planning and payments falling within category (a) should be avoided. Moreover, it may be advantageous if the employee is nearing retirement age for part of any compensation (perhaps the excess over the tax threshold of £30000 is appropriate) to be paid into the employee's pension scheme as a top-up payment. There is no tax charge on the amount contributed to the scheme and the employee will reap the benefit at a later stage.

From the employer's viewpoint

Perhaps more importantly for the employer is the question whether the payment made to the employee is deductible in ascertaining his own tax liability. The tax rules depend on a fine distinction as to whether the payment is regarded as a "capital" payment or "revenue" payment. Briefly the position is that payments made by way of damages or compensation for dismissal are normally fully deductible from profits in determining the employer's income tax liability. They are regarded as being "wholly and exclusively for the purposes of the trade".[33] Similar treatment is accorded to payments in lieu of notice and agreed compensation made under the contract of employment. Payments to an employee for a restrictive covenant were formerly not deductible as they were regarded as capital payments to preserve the goodwill of the business. Following section 73(2) of the Finance Act 1988 however, they are deductible in full from profits provided they are made on or after 9 June 1988.

---

[33] Within ICTA s.74.

INDEX

Statutes that appear in the index appear in bold.
Key cases in the index are in italics and other cases are referred to in the footnotes: these can be found by reference to the subject index below.

Advertisements 39–40
   discriminatory 49
Ageism 34–35
Agency staff 10–11
Agents 10
Appointments 42–43
Apportionment Act 1870 15
Apprenticeship 11, 13–14, 15
Attachment of earnings 141–144
Attachment of Earnings Act 1971 141, 142, 143, 144

Burdett-Coutts & others v *Hertfordshire County Council* 113, 116

Cadoux v *Central Regional Council* 54
Cars 24–25
Changes in terms 54, 108–127
Changes in working methods 96–99
Chell v *Hall and Boardman* 139–140
Coal Mines Regulation Act 1887 140
Collective agreements 5, 36, 37, 38, 50, 51, 54, 55
   and lay-off 87–88, 112
   and take-over 162
Commission for Racial Equality (CRE) 48, 49
Constructive dismissal 6, 7, 58, 65, 69, 114–115, 150, 151, 152, 154, 155–158
Consultants 4
Contract of employment 1, 4–6, 50–65, 106
   changing wages and 110–112, 113, 114
   deductions and 128–149
   equal pay and 123
   frustration of 163–166
   responsibilities during 66–107
   termination and 150–1, 166
Contract for services 1, 6, 106
Contract of service (*see* contract of employment)

Contractor (*see also* contractor for services) 1, 4, 6–8, 15, 76
Contractual obligation to pay wages 21–22
Court orders, payment of 141–144
Custom and practice 60–61

Deductions 67–68, 107, 128–149
    fixed 67–68
    authority to make 68
    retail workers and 134–140
Department of Employment 34, 36
Differentials 38
Direct discrimination (*see* sex discrimination, race discrimination)
Directors 9
    Discretionary payments 21, 22
Dismissal (*see also* constructive dismissal) 150, 151, 153–158
    in retailing 139–140

EEC nationals 35
Employee share schemes 28
Employment Act 1988 (EA) 147
Employment agencies 35, 144
Employment Agencies Act 1973 10, 35
Employment Protection Act 1975 2, 109, 119, 139
Employment Protection (Consolidation) Act 1978 (EPCA) 1, 5, 8, 11, 21, 52, 53, 54, 66, 68, 78, 79, 80, 87, 88, 89, 90, 91, 92, 98, 100, 101, 102, 103, 114, 115, 117, 150, 151, 152, 153, 154, 156, 158, 161
Employment relationships 3–14
    employer and contractor 6–10
    employer and employee 3–6
    principal and agent 10–11
    trainees 11–14
Employment Training 12–14
Engaging employees 3–49
Entitlement 22
Equal Opportunities Commission (EOC) 48, 49
Equal pay 5, 122–127
    defences against 126–127
    procedure 127
    variation of contract and 123–126
Equal Pay Act 1970 (EPA) 5, 44, 122, 123, 124, 125, 126, 127
Equivalent value 125
Expenses 6, 25, 105, 130
Express terms 51–55

Family Credit 106
Family members, as workers 9
Finance Act 1988 167, 168
Forms of wages 3, 19–32
Frustration of contract 163–166

Gibbons v *Associated British Ports* 111

Health insurance 71
Higher-paid employers 23, 24, 25, 27, 145
R. F. Hill v *Mooney* 18, 69, 111, 115
Holidays 6, 8, 27, 31, 52, 158
   and holiday pay 78–79, 84, 130, 159
   and notice 153–154
Homeworkers 9
Housing Benefit 106, 107

Implied terms 55–58
Income and Corporation Taxes Act 1988 (ICTA) 7, 23, 25, 26, 27, 28, 29, 30, 31, 167, 168
Income support 106, 107
Incorporation by reference 54
Independent contractors (*see* contractors)
Indirect discrimination (*see* racial discrimination, sexual discrimination)
Industrial action 91–95
   damages and 92–93
   deductions and 94–95, 133
   dismissal and 91–92, 154
   suspension and 93–94
Injury at work 71–72, 75–77, 154
Insolvency of employer (*see* termination)
Interest-free loans 27–28

Juries Act 1974 103
Jury service 103

Kent County Council v *Gilham* 118

Law Reform (Frustrated Contracts) Act 1943 166
Lay-off payments 2, 5, 84–91
Lethaby v *Horsman Andrew and Knill Ltd.* 140
Like work 124–125
Living accommodation 26
Local Government Finance Act 1982 64

Maintenance payments 67
Male comparator 125, 126
Maternity pay (*see* statutory maternity pay)
Medical insurance (*see* health insurance)
Medical suspension 78
Merchant Shipping Act 1970 131
Miles v *Wakefield District Council* 91, 95
Miller v *Harmworthy Engineering Ltd.* 112
Minimum guarantee payments 87, 89–91
Minimum wage 1

National Insurance 4, 6, 32, 76, 82, 83, 146–147
Negotiating pay 40–42
New technology 96–99
Notcutt v *Universal Equipment Co (London)* 164–165
Notices, workplace 58–59

Office holders 8–9, 95
Overpayment 103–104
   criminal liability and 105
   repayment and 132–133

Part-time staff 4
Patents Act 1977 106
Pay Board 64
Pay levels, fixing 34–39
   new businesses 35–37
   existing businesses 37–39
Pay offers 40–42
Pay statements 66–67, 68
Pay systems 3, 14–19
   flexibility and 5
Payment by results (PBR) 16–19
Penalty terms 14
Pensions 30–31, 52, 130, 143
   and employer's insolvency 160
   and sickness 76–77
Performance related pay (*see* payment by results)
Pickwell v *Camden London Borough Council* 64
Piecework 16, 120–121
Political levy 148–149
Pregnancy (*see also* statutory maternity pay) 73, 103
Profit related pay 29–30, 70
Profit related schemes 28–29

Public bodies 63–64
Public duties (*see* time off)

Race Relations Act 1976 43, 44, 45, 47, 48, 49, 121
Racial discrimination 34, 43–49, 121–2
    defences against 46–47
    employer's liability 47
    remedies for 48
Rainey v *Greater Glasgow Health Board* 126–127
Recruitment 33–149
Reduction in work (*see* lay-off)
Redundancy 6, 98–99, 102, 112, 131, 151, 158, 159, 160, 166–167
Reservists 103
Restrictive covenants 167
Retail workers 134–140
Retirement schemes 20–21
Rigby v *Ferodo Ltd.* 113, 116, 140
Roberts v *Hopwood and others* 64
Robertson v *British Gas Corporation* 54

Safety representatives 102
Sales staff 4
Self employment 7
Sex discrimination 34, 43–49
    defences against 46–47
    employer's liability for 47
    remedies 48
Sex Discrimination Act 1975 (SDA) 43, 44, 45, 47, 48, 49, 122
Sick pay (*see also* statutory sick pay) 6, 8, 52, 57, 58, 59, 71–72, 153–154, 158
Single-union arrangements 39
Social security (*see also* Family credit, Income Support, Housing Benefit) 2
Social Security Act 1986 2, 80
Social Security and Housing Benefits Act 1982 (SSHBA) 5, 72, 73, 74, 75
State Maternity Allowance 80
Statements of terms 52–53
Statutory Maternity Pay (SMP) 79–84, 130, 159
    period of 81
    qualifying conditions 80–81
    rates of 81–82
Statutory Sick Pay (SSP) 2, 5, 72–75, 76, 77, 130, 143, 159
    qualifying conditions 73

Suspension 93–94
  and new technology 97

Take-over (*see* transfer of undertaking)
Tax 2, 4, 6, 7, 144, 158
  implications for wages 20–32
  PAYE and 144–146
  SMP and 82
  sickness benefits and 77
  termination and 166–168
Temporary workers 4
Termination 150–168
  dismissal 153–158
  employer's insolvency 158–160
  frustration of contract 163–166
  taxation of payments 166–168
  transfer of undertaking 161–163
  voluntary 150–152
Territorial Army 103
Theft Act 1968 105
Time off 99–103
Time rates 16
Tips 20
Trade unions 1, 162
  changes in wages and 108–109
  paying subscriptions to 133, 147, 158
  time off and 100–102, 158, 159
Trade Union Act 1913 148
Trade Union Act 1984 148, 149
Trade Union and Labour Relations Act 1974 (TULRA) 55
Transfer of undertakings 161–163
Truck Acts 1831–1940 128, 129, 131

Unfair dismissal (*see* constructive dismissal)

Vouchers 26–27

Wages
  attachment of earnings and 143
  changing 108–127
  contract of service and 4
  contractual terms 50–65
  deductions and 128–149
  definition of/forms of 19–32
  delays in paying 68–69
  Employment Training and 13

    inadequate 14–15
    industrial action and 91–95
    new technology and 96–99
    responsibilities during contract and 66–107
    systems for determining 16
Wages Act 1986 (WA) 1, 5, 6, 68, 105, 119, 120, 121, 128, 129, 130, 131, 132, 133, 134, 135, 136, 137, 138, 139, 147, 148
Wages Council Act 1979 119
Wages council orders 1, 34, 119–121
Wages Inspectorate 34
Wages systems (*see* pay systems)
Wiltshire v *NATFHE and Guy* 151
Work of equal value 125–126
Wrongful dismissal 115

Youth Training Scheme (YTS) 12, 135

OTHER BOOKS FROM SHAW & SONS

Employer and Employee
G. Barrie Marsh

The third edition of Marsh's book takes into account the fast-changing state of industrial relations in the past ten years. This period has been one of rapid change in employment law, culminating in the Employment Act of 1988. Barrie Marsh is the Senior Partner of Mace & Jones, Liverpool and has built a reputation for himself and his firm as a leading authority on the practical legal problems resulting from employer-employee relations. This edition will reinforce that reputation. It is a complete and practical guide to modern employment law. Commencing with the advertisement for the job, it covers all the stages of the employment process including the especially problematic areas of contracts of employment, sick pay and dismissal. The work of the industrial tribunal is also covered. Written in an extremely accessible style, **Employer and Employee** will provide an excellent guide to lawyer, personnel officer, trade unionist, company director and academic alike.
ISBN 0 7219 0742 3   **1989**

Shaw's Directory of Courts
Edited by G. Morris

Published annually, this directory, essential to every Court and legal office, takes account of all changes in staff, sittings of courts, addresses, court code numbers and telephone numbers each year. Document Exchange and Rutland Exchange numbers are included where appropriate. Careful research is carried out to ensure its accuracy at the time of publication. Prison establishments, Crown Courts, County Courts, Magistrates'

Courts and other courts of summary jurisdiction are fully covered. An essential tool for any lawyer undertaking regular litigation.
ISBN 0 7219 0985 X

Private Prosecutions
Richard Stafford

The private prosecution has become an increasingly important feature of the criminal justice system, especially in the period since the CPS was formed. Recent cases have brought the private prosecution to the public's consciousness. Richard Stafford's book provides an important, and unique, study of the private prosecution. In addition to a general explanation of criminal liability and the investigation of crime, chapters are devoted to problems of particular interest to the lawyer: the decision to prosecute and recurring problems in private prosecutions. An important book for anyone wishing to take out a private prosecution or examine the feasibility of so doing.
ISBN 0 7219 1090 4

Hello, Good Evening and Welcome
John Brand

Deregulation of television and radio will soon be upon us. More and more professionals will find that acting as spokesmen and being interviewed on behalf of their organisation is an important part of their working life. This booklet is an ideal introduction to the skills needed and the techniques used to create a more interesting and newsworthy interview and present a positive contribution rather than being a passive interviewee. John Brand has extensive experience in radio and television and runs a training school designed to make trainees as effective as possible through these media.
ISBN 0 7219 0762 8